Taking God's Stuff God's Way

Stewardship Stories for Kids

Debbonnaire Kovacs

MW01124254

Taking Care of God's Stuff God's Way

Prepared by Stewardship Ministries
North American Division of Seventh-day Adventists
12501 Old Columbia Pike
Silver Spring, MD 20904
igivesda.org

Author: Debbonnaire Kovacs
Copy Editor: Amy Prindle
Cover Design & Illustrations: Ryan Choi
Layout: Nick Sharon

Available from
Advent*Source*
5120 Prescott Avenue
Lincoln, NE 68506
www.adventsource.org
402.486.8800

© 2013 North American Division Corporation of Seventh-day Adventists.
All rights reserved. No part of this book may be used or reproduced by
any means, graphic, electronic, or mechanical, including photocopying,
recording, taping or by any information storage retrieval system without
the written permission of the publisher except in the case of brief quota-
tions embodied in critical articles and reviews.

ISBN# 978-1-57756-040-1

Printed in the United States of America

Table of Contents

Storyteller's Introduction

This book contains 23 stewardship stories for children. They are intended for the designated children's section of the worship service, but may also be used for children's church, Sabbath School enrichment, Vacation Bible School, or any time children's stories are needed on this topic. The specific subject matter for these stories are taken from Fundamental Seventh-day Adventist Belief #21, which states:

> We are God's stewards, entrusted by Him with time and opportunities, abilities and possessions, and the blessings of the earth and its resources. We are responsible to Him for their proper use. We acknowledge God's ownership by faithful service to Him and our fellow men, and by returning tithes and giving offerings for the proclamation of His gospel and the support and growth of His church. Stewardship is a privilege given to us by God for nurture in love and the victory over selfishness and covetousness. The steward rejoices in the blessings that come to others as a result of his faithfulness. (Gen. 1:26-28; Gen. 2:15; 1 Chron. 29:14; Haggai 1:3-11; Mal. 3:8-12; 1 Cor. 9:9-14; Matt. 23:23; 2 Cor. 8:1-15; Rom. 15:26, 27.) [see www.adventist.org/beliefs]

These stories are intended for an age range of 2nd grade through 5th grade, but some can be easily adapted for other ages. Those which can be particularly useful for younger children are noted as such. Preschool children and younger may have only a rudimentary understanding of taking care of things for God, and may not yet associate the word "stewardship" with this practice.

There is a thought question at the end of each story. You may sometimes have time to ask the children for their responses. Most often, however, you will simply give them the question to think about, or to talk to their parents about later. Each story is planned to take close to five minutes. It can be shortened by simplifying it, or lengthened by further discussing the points in the story with your young listeners.

What Is Stewardship?

You might begin by asking the children if they know what this big word means. Tell them you'll ask again when the story is over.

For younger children, shorten the description of what a steward is and concentrate on the story of the dog taking care of things for the children. Explain that we can help to take care of things for Jesus.

"Joey, you're very quiet today!"

Mom turned her head and looked over her shoulder into the back seat of the car. Joey was gazing out the window, not saying anything.

"Is anything wrong?"

"No, I'm just wondering about something," said Joey. "Today in Sabbath School, the teacher was talking about stewards. She said a steward was like a caretaker. But I still don't really get it."

Dad chimed in. "Well, another word for a steward would be a manager. You know Joe's restaurant that we go to sometimes?"

"Yeah, I like their spaghetti!" said Joey.

"Well, we call it Joe's restaurant, but Joe doesn't really own it."

"I know, Dad, Mr. McIntyre owns it. He just hires Joe to take care of things. Oh, I get it! So Joe's a steward, right?"

"Right! And he has to make decisions about things based on what he knows Mr. McIntyre wants, not on what he wants himself. For example, I happen to know that Joe would like to hire another waiter, but Mr. McIntyre says he can't afford it."

"There are other kinds of stewards, too," Mom added. "Anybody who takes care of things for someone else is a steward. Joanna, who takes care of Grandma and helps her with her housework, is like a steward."

"How about when I take out the trash for you? Am I a steward?" Joey asked.

"Absolutely!" Mom smiled. "And stewardship for God is taking care of God's stuff God's way!"

"But everything is God's," Joey pointed out.

"Exactly!" said Mom.

Just then, Dad pulled the car into the driveway.

"Wow, what is that big, furry, black animal running to the fence?" he asked, trying to look surprised.

"It's almost like a bear!" exclaimed Mom, pretending to be scared.

Joey laughed and opened his door. "Hi, Buddy! Were you a good boy while we were gone?"

Joey ran over to his black dog, who was nearly as tall as he was. Buddy tried to "wash Joey's face by licking it. Joey giggled and turned his face away. "Quit, Buddy! I'm already clean—I cleaned up for church, remember?"

Buddy barked happily and ran for his ball.

"Not now, Buddy," said Mom. "Joey, go inside and wash off the doggy germs. It's time for Sabbath dinner, and the Nelsons are coming over."

The conversation during dinner was mostly about grown-up things, but Joey kept thinking about stewards. His Sabbath School teacher had said we could all be stewards for God. Joey thought he would like to be a good steward for God, but what could a kid take care of, besides taking out the trash and cleaning his room? That didn't count as taking care of God's stuff, did it?

The next morning, Joey woke up early. He put food in Buddy's bowl. While the dog gobbled his food, Joey got dressed and brushed his teeth. Then he put Buddy out in the fenced yard while he ate his own breakfast. Some of the kids were coming over to play ball today. Mom had said they could go to the park down the street where they wouldn't have to worry about their ball breaking any windows.

Joey helped to clear the table when he was finished eating.

"You're being a good steward today, Joey," said Mom.

Joey was surprised. "I am?"

"Yes. A good steward does his duties without having to be asked, and especially without having to be told over and over!"

Joey grinned. He knew there were times when he did have to be told over and over. "I'm trying to do better, Mom."

He got his bat and glove and hurried out. "Come on, Buddy! The others will be waiting for us!"

All the kids at the park put their jackets in a heap on the grass.

"Here, Buddy, watch these for us!" said Joey. Buddy lay down by the jackets and panted, his long, pink tongue hanging out of his mouth.

A little while later, just when Joey was about to make a home run, he heard Buddy bark. It distracted him, and Ben tagged him.

"Out!" yelled Lissa.

Joey hardly noticed. "What's the matter with Buddy?"

The dog was standing up beside the pile of jackets, barking fiercely. All the kids ran over, just in time to see some older boys running around the corner. One jacket lay on the ground over on the sidewalk. Buddy stopped barking long enough to go pick up the jacket in his teeth and bring it back to the pile. Then he sat down and panted again, looking like he was grinning.

"Wow!" exclaimed Ben. "Did you see that? Those guys tried to take my jacket!"

"But Buddy stopped them!" said Joey proudly. "Maybe they would have taken them all."

"I heard those kids took some stuff and burned it last week!" added Lissa.

"Wow, Buddy, good dog!" All the kids hugged and petted Buddy while he smiled his drooly grin.

"Let's go to my house, I don't want to play anymore," said Joey. "I want to tell my dad about this!"

They picked up their balls, bats, gloves, and jackets, and trooped down the street to Joey's house. Dad was outside mowing, but he stopped long enough to hear the kids' excited story.

"Well, Buddy, you were a good steward today!" he said, patting Buddy's furry head.

"Yeah! That's exactly what he was!" cried Joey.

"What's a steward?" asked Kenji.

Joey smiled. "A steward is someone who takes care of things for someone else. Buddy took care of our jackets, even though he doesn't even know why we need them. He just did it because he loves us!"

Joey looked back down at Buddy. "You have your own fur coat, don't you, boy?"

Then Ben asked, "What about when I take care of my little brothers and sisters? Is that being a steward?"

"Yep!"

"Our school books!" said Lissa. "We have to take really good care of them because they don't belong to us."

"Right, and library books," added Kenji.

"You can learn a lot from a dog!" said Joey, rubbing Buddy's ears.

 Thought Question: *If stewardship is taking care of God's stuff God's way, what are some of the things you help to take care of for God?*

What is Stewardship? 2

You might begin by asking the children if they know what this big word means. Tell them you'll ask again when the story is over. Also, in this story, you may choose to let your listeners engage in the story's discussion about Zacchaeus for themselves.

This story is well suited to children of most ages.

Destiny was so excited! She was in the 2nd grade now, and today was the first day she got to be Teacher's Helper. Not just any kid could be Teacher's Helper. You had to earn it. Destiny had done all her homework and remembered to be quiet when Ms. Dean was talking, and yesterday she'd helped the new boy, Shawn, to find all the supplies he needed at art time. So Ms. Dean had said, "Destiny, tomorrow you may be my Helper." And now the day had come!

"What shall I do first, Ms. Dean?" she asked eagerly.

"How would you like to write, 'Good morning, boys and girls!' on the white board?"

Destiny's heart was beating a little faster than usual. She chose the red dry-erase marker and used her very best handwriting to make the greeting really big, so you could see it from the very back row.

"Perfect!" said Ms. Dean. "Now you may pass out these coloring pictures to all the students. Class, Destiny is passing out some pictures for you to color while I read our Bible lesson. Can anyone tell me who this is in the picture?"

Destiny knew the answer, but she let the other kids hold up their hands. She was busy being the Teacher's Helper.

Dawn, who was sometimes a little clumsy, dropped her picture on the floor and it slid under Anthony's desk. "I'll get it!" said Destiny. She retrieved the picture and gave it back to Dawn with a smile.

"It's Zacchaeus in the tree!" said Anthony.

"Right! While you are coloring your picture, I want you to listen carefully to the story, and then we'll talk about it."

Destiny finished passing out pictures and sat at her desk to color while Ms. Dean read. It was one of her favorite stories. She knew that she would have climbed a tree to see Jesus!

After Jesus told Zacchaeus He was going to his house that day, and Zacchaeus said he would pay back all the money he'd taken and even four times more, she lifted her head for her second favorite part (after the tree). Ms. Dean looked around at her class and said, "Then Jesus said, 'Today, salvation has come to this house!'"

Destiny loved that!

"Now, children, here's my question for you: Do you think Zacchaeus was a good steward?"

"What's a steward again?" asked Dawn. "I forget."

"That's all right, Dawn," Ms. Dean reassured her. "Can anyone help Dawn to remember?"

Destiny raised her hand, but William was called on.

"It's somebody who takes care of stuff."

"Their own stuff?" asked Ms. Dean.

"No!" said Anthony, forgetting to raise his hand. "Other people's stuff!"

"I remember!" said Dawn. "It's like a manager, right?"

"Right! So was Zacchaeus a good manager?"

"Well, he managed his own money for himself," Leo pointed out.

"You mean he managed other people's money for himself!" said Destiny.

"Yeah, I think he was a bad steward," said Dawn, and all the kids agreed.

"And then what happened?" asked Ms. Dean.

"Jesus came!" the children chorused.

"That changes everything," said Destiny.

"Always!" Ms. Dean agreed, smiling. "What changed for Zacchaeus?"

"He gave a bunch of money away!" said William. "How is that being a good manager?"

"It wasn't his money in the first place!" Destiny pointed out. "Giving it back is not the same as giving it away."

"And anyway," said Cindy, "part of being a good steward of God's money is giving it away to people who need it."

"Here's the main thing we have to remember about being a steward," said Ms. Dean. "An owner takes care of his or her own things—money, possessions like a car or a house or clothes, time, health…all of that, right?"

"Right," said all the children.

"An owner might take good care of things or might take bad care of things. But a steward needs to take extra specially good care of the things he or she is caring for, because they belong to someone else. If a steward doesn't take good care of things, what do you think might happen?"

"He'll get fired!" said William.

"Now tell me this: Who owns your house and car?"

"My dad," said one.

"My mom," said another.

"I do!" said Anthony, and everybody laughed.

Ms. Dean laughed, too, but she didn't say anything. And the kids knew by the look on her face that they didn't quite have the right answer yet.

"God does," said Destiny.

Ms. Dean smiled. "And who owns your clothes, your food, and your money?"

"God does!" all the children answered.

"Who owns you?"

"God does! And stewardship is taking care of God's stuff God's way!"

Destiny hardly heard the chorus of answers. She was thinking about something. Suddenly she raised her hand.

"Yes, Destiny?"

"When I'm Teacher's Helper, and I get to pass things out and clean the boards at the end of the day, and all that..." she hesitated.

"Yes?"

"Well...am I really God's Helper?" Destiny held her breath. She felt kind of funny even asking.

"Good question!" said Ms. Dean. "Children, what do you think?"

"God owns the white board!" one said.

"God owns the markers!" called another.

"God owns the whole school!" said Dawn.

"And...God owns me!" said Destiny. "I'm going to be the very best Teacher's Helper and God's Helper I can be!"

 Thought Question*: How can you be a good helper for God and take care of His stuff His way?*

Great-Grandma Ellen & the Nursing Home

Begin by saying something like this: "God owns everything, and stewardship is taking care of God's stuff God's way. One of the things He gives us to take care of is time. We think of it as our time, but of course it's God's time. Today's story is about a boy who is learning how to use time God's way."

To adapt for younger children, shorten and simplify, and perhaps have Jaden tell stories to Great-Grandma instead of reading them.

Jaden was very worried when he came home from school one afternoon and found Mom crying. He dropped his backpack on the floor and went to sit by her on the couch.

"Mom! What's wrong?"

Mom blew her nose and wiped her eyes. "Sorry to alarm you, Jaden. I didn't know how late it was. I'm fine, it's just that...well, you know how Great-Grandma Ellen had to go to the hospital when she fell, and then she got sick, and now she's been there two weeks?"

"Yeah."

"Well, the doctor says she can't live at home by herself anymore. But that's not the worst part. She can't come to live with us, either, or with Grandma Jean. The doctor says she needs special care, and she'll have to live in a nursing home. And I didn't want her to have to live in a nursing home!" Mom's eyes filled with tears again.

Jaden didn't know what to do or say. He'd been in the nursing home a few times, visiting people and singing to them with his Sabbath School class. He didn't like it there. It smelled funny, and the people were old—not like Grandma Jean, who sometimes still played ball with him and his brothers. Not even like Great-Grandma Ellen, who told the best stories in the world. No, those people were really old! They sat in wheelchairs or pulled themselves around with their feet. They looked at you funny, or they didn't look at you at all, and they might say strange things. It was kind of scary.

Jaden knew God loved all those people, of course, and he did like singing to them, especially when some of them sang along in their old, crackle-y voices. He liked to think about Jesus coming, and making them all young and strong again. No more wheelchairs or crutches after that happens!!

But to have his own Great-Grandma Ellen living there, he thought that would be awful. She wouldn't be able to make cookies anymore. Maybe she wouldn't even be able to tell stories. What if she had to sit in a wheelchair all the time, or couldn't get up at all? Some of the old people there never got out of their beds.

The doorbell rang, and then Grandma Jean came in. She sat down between Mom and Jaden and put her arms around both of them. Mom put her head on Grandma Jean's shoulder, just as if she were a little kid.

"Listen," said Grandma Jean. "We found a great nursing home, right here in town. We'll be able to go see her every day. She'll be fine! We'll pray with her, and as soon as she is stronger, we'll take her to church with us."

Jaden didn't say anything, but he was thinking, Every day? I have school, and homework, and ball practice, and I'm supposed to practice my clarinet. Now I have to go to a nursing home every single day?

A few weeks passed. The grown-ups seemed to be all in a flurry all the time. They had to pack up all Great-Grandma Ellen's stuff (she had a lot of stuff!) and try to figure out which of those things she could fit into the little room she had to share with another lady. They talked to lawyers and bankers and the people who ran the nursing home, and had noisy discussions (sometimes more like arguments, Jaden thought) around the dining room table or on the phone.

Jaden tried to help sometimes, and he learned not to mind going to visit Great-Grandma Ellen in her room, although he liked it best when the other lady wasn't in there. But mostly, he stayed busy with his own stuff. He felt kind of guilty inside, but he didn't say anything about that. At night, he would ask God to bless Great-Grandma Ellen. Then he would get into bed quickly and try to think about his next ballgame, or what computer game he could play with his brothers the next day.

One day Dad said, "Hey, buddy, I have a great idea! Great-Grandma's eyes are getting bad, you know, and she can't read very well for herself. You know how much she always loved to read. She used to read to you boys all the time, remember?"

Yes, Jaden remembered. Her stories, whether read or told, were what he missed most. (Well, and her cookies!) He nodded to Dad reluctantly.

"Now's your chance to return the favor," said Dad. "I thought you could go for an hour or so a few times a week and read to her. You're getting really good at reading. She'd love that!"

"But I don't have time!" protested Jaden.

Dad looked surprised. "Really? How much time does God give you?"

Jaden wrinkled his forehead. "What?"

Dad smiled and joked, "Well, God gives me 24 hours every day, and I thought that was the same for everybody, but maybe you don't get that many?"

Jaden knew Dad was trying to make him laugh, but he frowned instead. "You know what I mean! I have homework and ball practice, and I'm teaching Jimmy to ride his bike, and I've got to learn that clarinet solo for the school concert…"

"You always have enough time for other people," said Dad. "There's Sabbath afternoon. That's always free. Couldn't you find one or two other times in the week when you could give her an hour?"

Jaden hung his head, and Dad put his arm around his shoulders and said, "It's kind of like tithe, Jaden. You take out God's share first, and the rest goes further. True stewardship is taking care of God's stuff, including time, God's way. Time you give to someone who needs you is time you give to Jesus."

"It is?" asked Jaden. He hadn't thought of it that way before. He knew that his friends were always complaining that their allowances weren't big enough, but they were usually bigger than his, and he had enough for what he really needed, even after tithe. Could God make his time stretch like that?

"I'll think about it," he said. And that night he made some plans. If he went on Monday after school for one hour, and on Wednesday after supper, that wouldn't interfere with his music or lessons or ballgames. He usually had the most homework later in the week, and if something came up that was really important, he could switch things around. He could even read her a book he was already reading—Great-Grandma had always liked the same kind of stories he liked, especially ones about horses.

That Sabbath afternoon, Jaden sat on the edge of Great-Grandma Ellen's bed and read her the first chapter of A Horse and a Hat and a Big, Wet Splat. Her eyes lit up as they hadn't in quite a long time. And Jaden's heart felt better than it had in a long time, too.

 Thought Question*: What are some ways you can use your time for God and others, and manage His time His way?*

There Is a Time for Everything

Begin by saying something like this: "God owns everything, and stewardship is taking care of God's stuff God's way. One of the things He gives us to take care of is time. We think of it as our time, but of course it's God's time. Today's story is about a girl who is learning how to use time God's way."

This story is better suited for school-age children.

It was Friday afternoon, and church school let out early. Jenisha ran into the house laughing, and dropped her backpack on the floor by the door.

"Jenisha…" said Mom with a sigh.

"I know, I know! Sorry, Mom! I'll pick it up in a minute, but guess what!" Jenisha bounced into the kitchen where her mother was making special food for Sabbath. "We have a special project in social studies. It's due on Monday, and Kane and Jill and Ming and I are supposed to work together on it. We're going to make a salt dough map of our whole state! Kane's drawing the outline this evening at his house, and then we're going to go over there and figure out where all the cities go and stuff, and Jill's going to paint the rivers and make different colors of green and brown for hills and mountains, and Ming will print all the words, because she has the best handwriting you ever saw, but before all that—"

"Wait, wait, wait!" said Mom. "You're talking too fast and making me dizzy! Was that all one sentence?"

Jenisha laughed. "Yeah, and first, before all that, I mean after the outline, but before all the painting and stuff, we have to make the state, and make all the hills, and can you make the salt dough? I promised you would."

"I'll help you make it," said Mom. "But first, pick up your book bag and put it away, then wash your hands and set the table for supper. Then we'll talk."

"Okay!"

While Jenisha was upstairs, the phone rang. "I'll get it, Mom!" she said excitedly. It was her friend who went to a different school, so she had to tell the whole story all over again. Mom had called to Jenisha three times before she finally came down to set the table, and she finished in a hurry just as her two big brothers came in the door, followed shortly by Dad.

At supper, Jenisha excitedly told the rest of the family all about her project. Mom promised that she and Jenisha would make the dough right after the supper dishes were washed.

"I have to go next door to Nora's first," said Jenisha.

"What do you mean you have to go to Nora's? I thought you said you were going to Kane's to work on your project."

"We are, but she called while I was upstairs, and she has a new puppy and I promised to go see it. It's only for a few minutes, and then I'll come and help with the dishes and the dough and everything, and I know I can be at Kane's by 7."

"I don't think—" said Mom, but Jenisha was already out the door.

A whole hour passed before she got back, and Mom had already done all the dishes. "Sorry I'm late!" said Jenisha. "The puppy was so cute! Did you make the salt dough yet?"

"No, I did not," said Mom, and Jenisha knew she was in trouble. Quickly she said, "It's okay, I'll do it, I'm ready now."

Mom sighed, and took her into the kitchen, where they made a big bowl of salt dough. "Now, here's a wet towel to cover it with, but you have to use it right away," said Mom. "I'll call Kane's mom to let her know you're on your way, and Dad can drive you over."

At Kane's house, the four kids started on the map, but they had so much fun goofing off and putting salt dough on each other that the dough started to dry before they finished. They ended up doing a bit of a messy job. Ming was upset, because she wanted it to be perfect.

"I'm taking it to my house to fix it and make it better by Sunday," she said.

Sabbath was fun, as always, and in the evening after worship, Jenisha watched her favorite TV show, ate popcorn and apples, played a computer game with her brothers, and got to bed late. She meant to call Ming, but she never got around to it.

Sunday morning was bright and sunny. Mom gave Jenisha permission to ride her bike to Ming's house. But on the way, Jenisha found some friends at the park, and played on the swings and monkey bars just for a little while. At least, she meant for it to be just a little while, but before she knew it, her stomach was telling her it was lunch time. She hurriedly rode to Ming's house, because Ming's mom had promised lunch to the social studies team.

The kids seemed pretty mad when she got there. "Where have you been? We've already got almost all the painting done, and Ming's started labeling the cities!" said Kane.

The map was looking pretty good without much help from her, to tell the truth. Jenisha apologized to her friends and tried to paint one particularly long river without messing it up. It was hard painting in all those little wiggles and wide places.

"Here," said Jill, "do this lake in blue—paler blue around the outside and darker in the middle where it's deeper. Did you do your paper already?"

Jenisha gasped. "My paper! I forgot! I was looking forward to doing the map so much I totally forgot we had to write papers, too! Mine was about the main products of the state, right?"

Kane gave her a disgusted look. "No, mine was about the products, you were supposed to do one on the history! How are you going to get that done now? This is due tomorrow, and all our grades are going to be worse because of you!"

Jenisha felt like crying. She knew it was true. All her friends were going to pay the penalty of her actions.

"Listen," said Jill, who always made peace if she could. "Jenisha did make the salt dough and did some molding and some painting. Why don't we let her go home now and do her paper? We can finish the rest."

"Oh, all right," the others grumbled.

So Jenisha, not laughing or smiling, apologized again and rode home.

Dad met her at the door. "You're not looking very happy," he said.

"I feel bad, Daddy. I didn't get to do much of the fun stuff, and I forgot all about a two-page paper I have to write about the history of the state! The others have all done their papers, and they sent me home to do mine, but I have to hurry now, and it won't be very good."

Dad hugged her. "Well, you know our saying, right? 'First work and then play...'"

"I know, '...makes you happy all the day.' It's even worse when the work you're putting off is fun itself, and almost like play! Dad, will you pray that God will help me take care of His time His way?"

"Of course," said Dad, and they prayed together. Then he helped Jenisha look up the history facts she needed, and together they made a schedule which she tacked on her wall. At the top it said, "There is a time for everything. There's a time for everything that is done on earth" (Ecclesiastes 3:1, NIRV).

"I'll pray about it every day, Daddy. Jesus will help me do better, I know He will!" said Jenisha. And Jesus is helping her every day.

 Thought Question: *What are some ways you could improve your management of God's time God's way?*

If I Couldn't Sing

You might begin by asking children if there is something they're especially good at, and that they like doing. Encourage them to say all kinds of things, from music and drawing to running, math, reading, helping people, whatever. Then say something like, "God has given us all talents and gifts. Our abilities actually belong to Him, and stewardship is taking care of God's gifts in God's way. Today's story is about a boy who is learning to take care of his gift for God."

This story is better suited for school-age children.

One of Kenny's Grandma's friends came to talk to him. "Well hello, Kenny, how old are you?"

Kenny didn't really like it when grown-ups talked to him like this, but he was polite. "Nine, ma'am."

"Nine! Well, aren't you a grown up little man!"

Yuck, that was even worse. And Kenny knew what was coming next.

"What are you going to do when you grow up?"

He used to say, "I don't know," after which the grown-up would usually say something like, "Do you want to be a fireman, or a cowboy?" Kenny thought that kind of stuff was for kindergarteners. But he had recently decided exactly what he wanted to do, so this time he said, "I'm going to be a famous singer!"

Grandma's friend looked surprised. "Oh, really! So you can sing?"

"Oh, can he sing!" Grandma chimed in. "I've been putting him in front of people to sing since he was three or four years old! He used to be shy, but not anymore. Wait till you hear him sing. Maybe he'll sing for us after supper."

Kenny had made up his own song this time, and he was proud of it. It was about a boy and his dog. After supper, he sang his song for Grandma and her friends, and they clapped and said what a good singer he was. That was the part he liked. He wanted to be like one of the guys he saw on youtube at his friends' houses, with a band and some girls singing backup. He was also planning on learning the electric guitar.

That evening at bedtime, Grandma sat on the end of Kenny's bed and said, "Kenny, I want to talk to you about something. You know I like your singing and that I think you can do something great with it, right?"

"Yeah, Grandma, and thanks for helping me my whole life. When I'm famous and rich, I'll buy you a new house and a big, fancy car."

Grandma looked troubled. "Well, that's just it, Kenny. Lately, I'm a little worried by the way you talk. I don't think God gave you the gift of singing just so you could get rich and famous."

Kenny frowned. "He gave it to me, right? It's my gift, to do what I want with it."

Grandma looked almost shocked. "Kenny, God gives us gifts to use for Him, not for ourselves!"

"But I'm not going to use it just for myself! Didn't I just say I'm going to get you a new house?"

"I don't need a new house. Jesus will be coming soon, you know. What about singing for His glory?"

Kenny sighed. "Don't worry, Grandma, I'm not going to sing anything bad, or do drugs, or anything like that. I know some of the big singers do some pretty bad things. I'm not going to sing in a hard rock band, you know. Didn't you like my song tonight? It wasn't about God, but it was a good song, right?"

"Sure, it was a nice song. I'm not saying you have to sing only church songs. I'm just saying you need to think about this, and pray about it, and always put God and His will first, before everything else. Riches and fame aren't necessarily bad things, but when you're older you'll understand that they can be dangerous, and those things alone are not a good reason for doing anything."

Kenny was not mad, exactly, but he was kind of annoyed. Grandma was old, he thought, and she just didn't understand. "I do pray about it, Grandma." He said as he lay down on his bed. "I'm kind of tired now."

Grandma kissed his forehead and left his room. He could tell that she was still worried about him.

At school the next day, Kenny talked to his best friend, Donny, about it.

"She just doesn't get it!" said Donny. "Wait till you're big news, then she'll be glad. And I get to be your drummer, right?"

"Sure, I promised, didn't I?" said Kenny. But secretly, he was afraid Donny might not be good enough. His rhythm wasn't always right on. When they got older, maybe Donny would lose interest. Or maybe Kenny would have to break it to him that he needed somebody more—what was that word? More professional? That was it. He did feel a little guilty, thinking this way about his friends and his future. It was like he was being disloyal to his friend. But singing was a business, after all. It wasn't personal.

That night, when he passed Grandma's door, he heard her praying out loud. She was saying, "Please, God, guide Kenny. I know You gave him his beautiful singing voice, and I know You have a plan for him. Please forgive me if I've made him proud. Maybe instead of encouraging him, I've helped him to get a big head and be selfish."

Was that a sniffle he heard? Was Grandma crying?

Kenny went to his room and thought very hard. Was he selfish? It didn't seem fair! People liked to hear him sing! That was okay, wasn't it? Wasn't it good that he wanted to buy his grandma a nice, new house? Still, he knew the gift of singing came from God and also ultimately belonged to God. Standing by his window, looking up at the starry sky, Kenny whispered, "Dear God, I only want to please You. I don't want to be selfish or have a big head. I want to take care of Your gifts Your way. Help me, please."

A few days later, Kenny started working on a new song. It didn't come easily, like the one about the boy and his dog, but even though it took longer, he felt really good about it afterward. It was kind of a prayer song. Kenny found that he talked best through singing, and he wanted to sing a request to God to help him be exactly what God wanted. "If You took away my voice, Lord, I'd still want you in my heart," he sang quietly to himself while he biked to school. Heart, art, part…what would be a good rhyme that would say what he wanted?

Finally he had it.

> *"If I couldn't sing, God, if I couldn't say a word,*
>
> *The only thing I'd want is for You to be my Lord."*

This new song had three verses. One thanked God for the gift of song. One asked God to help him be true. In the last verse, Kenny gave his heart, his life—and yes, his singing—to Jesus for Him to keep.

He felt shy, for the first time in ages, when he sang it for Grandma. She liked it so much she cried—old ladies were funny that way. "Kenny, I'm going to put this on the church's website!" said Grandma, hugging him so hard he thought his ribs would crack.

He had to sing it again, into her computer microphone. Then Grandma uploaded it onto the church website, and put a notice on the church Facebook page. The next day, the website had seventeen messages.

"Thank you, Kenny! But more than that, thank You, God!"

"Your song blessed me today, Kenny!"

"I am praying for you to always be true to God, Kenny. I know God has a plan for you. Maybe you'll help other people to love God, too!"

But the best message of all said, "Kenny, you don't know me. I've been watching this church website for a while. I like your preacher's sermons. I've been thinking of coming back to church, but I couldn't decide. Then I heard your song, and I'm giving my life back to God. Thank you, Kenny, for dedicating your life and your gift to God."

Grandma cried again, but you could tell she was really happy. And truthfully, Kenny got a little tearful, too!

 Thought Question: *What gift has God given you, and how are you going to use His gift His way?*

I-N-V-E-N-T-I-O-N

You might begin by asking children if there is something they're especially good at, and that they like doing. Encourage them to say all kinds of things, from music and drawing to running, math, reading, helping people, whatever. Then say something like, "God has given us all our talents and gifts. Our abilities actually belong to Him, and stewardship is taking care of God's gifts God's way. Today's story is about a girl who is learning what her gift is, and how to take care of it God's way."

Extra note*—you may also make flash cards of the words "separate," "intention," and "invention" to help with the last part of the story.*

This story is better suited for school-age children.

Margie leaned over the third grade art table to look at Anna's painting. "Your clouds look so real, Anna! How do you do that?"

"Well, I just kind of dabble the brush around the edges, like this."

Anna demonstrated, but when Margie tried it on hers, it just made the clouds look streaky and weird.

Anna leaned over and looked at Margie's. "Also, clouds aren't really all white, you know. There's a little bit of gray, and a little bit of blue, and sometimes even a tiny bit of pink."

Leo, at the other end of the table, said, "Don't worry, Margie, yours look better than mine!" He held up a picture of a dinosaur that looked just fine to Margie.

She knew Leo always tried to make other people feel better if he could. The truth was, her painting looked like it had been done by a two-year-old.

Margie sighed and did her best to finish. Art was the last class of the day. She liked it, but she just wasn't good at it!

Mrs. Donaldson had them all stand up and sing a good-bye song together before the end of the day. Margie could hear her voice squeaking as usual, and tried to sing quietly. Gordon and Sadie, who stood on either side of her, sounded so good—almost like grown-ups. She wished she could sing like that.

When they got outside, the whole class broke into a run, which was strictly against the rules. Mrs. King, the principal, shouted above the ruckus for them to slow down, and some of the parents who were waiting to take them home grabbed their kids out of the race. As usual, Pedro was at the front of the line, reaching his dad's car laughing.

And as usual, Margie was at the very back. In fact, she hardly even got started, because Mrs. Donaldson reached out and caught her. "Margie, you children know that running out here is dangerous where all the cars are!"

It wasn't Margie's fault! She didn't start the race.

In the back seat of her parents' station wagon, Margie was glum. Her eyebrows were scrunched together and her lower lip stuck out.

"What's the matter with you?" asked her big sister, Millie, who was in 5th grade (practically grown up).

"I can't do anything!" said Margie.

"What's that supposed to mean? You can do all sorts of stuff," said Millie.

"Nothing that counts," said Margie, still frowning. "Anna can paint like some kind of famous artist. You should see her skies. Did you know clouds have all kinds of colors in them besides white? And Sadie and Gordon can sing good enough to be on TV."

"Well enough," said Mom from the front seat.

"See?" wailed Margie. "I can't even talk right! Pedro runs so fast he can probably be in the Olympics someday. Even Leo, he's really good at making people feel better. I can't do anything!"

The whole rest of the way home, Margie listened half-heartedly while Mom and Millie tried to convince her that the fact that she kept her room clean, or helped with the supper dishes without being asked, or dumb stuff like that, was a gift. "It's even in the Bible," said Mom. "I'll show you this evening. It's called the gift of helps, and it's a gift of the Holy Spirit."

"It is?" Secretly, Margie was kind of impressed by that. But she still wished she could do something well that really meant something to lots of people.

That night, after they helped do the dishes and put away all the leftovers, she and Millie spread out their books on the clean table. Margie worked away at her math, which she didn't like, and read the next chapter in her reading book, which she loved. This book had stories about children in other countries, and it was very interesting.

After a while, she heard Millie sigh. Margie looked up from her book. "What's the matter?"

"I have a spelling test tomorrow, and I'm so horrible at spelling! It's one thing if the words are spelled like they sound. But English words are so confusing! Mrs. Petty says lots of our words come from other languages, and that's why. But I just hate it!"

"Spelling's not that hard," said Margie. "Let me see."

She put her book down and went to Millie's side of the table. "Separate. That one has a rat in the middle, did you know?"

"What?" Millie leaned closer to the book.

"See? S-E-P, sep, then, a rat, and then an E to make the A say its name."

"Cool!" said Millie. She shut her eyes. "S-E-P, umm, A-R-A-T-E!" She opened her eyes. "Right?"

"Right!" said Margie. "And two of these words have shun in them, which is spelled T-I-O-N. See, intention is I-N, in, then T-E-N, ten, then T-I-O-N, which sounds like 'shun'. Get it?"

"Yeah! So invention is, wait, don't tell me—" Millie shut her eyes again—"I-N-V-E-N-T-I-O-N." She opened her eyes. "Right? Yay! Wow, you're good at this, Margie. I bet it's because you read so much. Will you go over all these words with me?"

"Of course I will!" Margie bent over Millie's 5th grade spelling book and gave her sister advice and hints on every single word. She had her write them several times. "That helps you to remember them—not just in your mind, but in your hand."

Then she took the spelling book and sat across the table. "Okay. Here we go. Ready? Your first word is jealous." Margie tried to think of a sentence, the way Mrs. Donaldson always did. She laughed suddenly. "The girl was jealous of her friends' talents!"

Millie laughed, too. "Jealous. J-E-A-L. . . umm, wait a minute, don't tell me, oh yeah! O-U-S. Jealous."

"Correct!" said Margie. "This is great! I feel just like a teacher!"

"Hey, good idea!" said Millie. "I bet you'd be a great teacher!"

Margie felt good all over. "Maybe I will! Ready for your second word? Intention. I have every intention of helping you spell!"

The sisters gave each other high fives and laughed together.

Millie got a B+ on her spelling test the next day. She gave the test paper to Margie to hang in her room. "Now you know your gift! Don't forget, stewardship is taking care of God's stuff God's way, and that includes your ability to spell. And teach!" Millie gave her little sister a hug. "And thank you!"

 Thought Question: How can you use your abilities to help others and use God's gifts God's way?

Dear Friend

You might begin by saying something like, "Who gave us every single thing we have? Right, God did! Even our toys! Did you know our toys are really God's toys? We belong to God and everything we have belongs to God. Stewardship is taking care of God's stuff God's way. Here is a story about a boy who wants to take care of his toys God's way."

This story is well-suited for children of any age. For "the hills," you may substitute any appropriate mission area for your circumstances, or a foreign mission.

One Sabbath at church, Benjamin heard Mrs. Courtney say that she was going to visit the families who lived in the nearby hills. Benjamin knew she had done this before. He always liked to listen to the stories Mrs. Courtney told when she got back. Lots of the people who lived in the hills were very poor. They might not even have windows in their houses, and their clothes were ragged and thin. "Today," Mrs. Courtney said, "I have a special job for the children."

Benjamin sat up straighter. Was there something he could do to help those children who didn't have enough to eat?

"Most of the children," Mrs. Courtney explained, "don't have any toys. Or maybe they have one old rusty truck or one ragged doll. I saw one family where the children were playing catch with a ball made out of rags."

Benjamin's mouth dropped open and he looked up at his mom. No toys at all? A ball made of rags?

"So here's how I'd like you children to help me. I want to take a whole carload of toys back to these families when I go. Will you look through your toys and see if you have some nice ones you'd like to share with the children that I visit? They can't be computer games, or things like that. They shouldn't need batteries or electricity. And they need to be nice. We wouldn't want to give them old, worn-out things. For one thing, that's what they already have, and for another, we want them to know Jesus loves them, and this is one way to tell them that."

Benjamin had never thought about that before. In the car, he asked his daddy, "Does having toys tell me Jesus loves me?"

"Well, think of it this way," said Daddy. "When you give somebody a present, what are you trying to say to them?"

Benjamin thought about it. "That I love them and want them to be happy?"

"Exactly. So when you give something to somebody, and you do it with love, that's one way of saying you love them, and it's also one way to share Jesus' love with them. Also, everything we own came from God and belongs to God, anyway. So in a way, we're just sharing God's own toys with some of His other kids."

"That's cool!" said Benjamin. "I want to send some of my toys—I mean, God's toys—to the kids in the hills."

The next day, Mom and Benjamin went through his toy box. "Here's my old fire truck," he said. "I don't really need that anymore."

"Is that the kind of present you'd like to get?" asked Mom.

"Oh, yeah," said Benjamin. "I forgot we were trying to give away the best stuff. What about this football? It's practically new, and those kids only have balls made out of rags!"

"Good choice," said Mom, putting the football into a bag. "What else?"

"How about some books?" Benjamin went to his bookshelf. He hesitated over some of his favorite ones, but he didn't like the idea of other kids like him not having any books at all. "Some of them are a little faded because I've looked at them a lot, but the stories are still good. Like this one of Bible stories. I want to give them that one, Mom. Do you think it would be okay?"

"I think it would be great," said Mom. "Maybe we can clean them up and make them look a little nicer. Is that all?"

"Hmm…no." Benjamin looked around his room. He had a lot of toys! Most of them just sat there; he couldn't play with them all! He found some more balls, piled up some of his best stuffed toys, and looked over his action figures for the ones that were the nicest.

But there was one thing that kept coming back to his mind again and again. More than anything in the world, Benjamin loved building things. He had had blocks and things when he was smaller, but one of his friends had a really cool set that would build skyscrapers and robots and airplanes and castles, and all kinds of stuff. Benjamin had wanted a set like that for a long time, and finally, for his birthday, Mom and Daddy had bought him one. Benjamin had even saved up some of the money himself.

He looked at Mom. "What about my building set?"

Mom looked surprised. "You don't have to give away all your favorite things!" she said.

"I know," said Benjamin. "But I keep thinking about a kid who maybe is my age, and doesn't have enough food or clothes, and maybe he wants to be a builder like me. And I can still play with Jerry's, you know. He doesn't care. It's kind of more fun to do it together, anyway. I can save more money and buy another set later, but maybe that kid would never have one if I don't give him one!"

"I am very proud of you, Benjamin Joseph," said Mom. Her eyes were glistening.

"I want to write a letter, too," said Benjamin. "Will you help me spell stuff?"

"Of course I will."

Mom gave Benjamin some paper, and he began. "Dear…who do I say? Dear Boy? Or I guess it could be a girl, too, huh, Mom?"

"How about 'Dear Friend,'" suggested Mom.

"Dear Friend,

I hope you like this building set. It is my favorite in the whole world. My dad says it really belongs to God, so I want to share it with you, because I want to take care of God's stuff God's way. Please take good care of it. Maybe you could send me a picture of what you build.

Your friend, Benjamin."

"Hey, Mom! Do you think I could find out who gets it? Maybe we could be friends! How far away are the hills, anyway?"

Mom smiled. "We'll talk to Mrs. Courtney about it. If she says it's okay, we'll write our address on the letter, so whoever gets the set can write back to you."

She gave Benjamin a hug. "I am very proud of you! And so is Jesus! I think you are taking great care of His toys for Him!"

 Thought Question*: Have you ever thought of your toys as belonging to God? How are you doing at taking care of them His way?*

A Trip to Aunt Sarah's

You might begin by saying something like, "Who gave us every single thing we have? Right, God did! We belong to God, and everything we have belongs to God. Stewardship is taking care of God's stuff God's way. Here is a story about a girl who wants to learn to take care of herself and her things God's way."

This story may be simplified for younger children.

"Kaylee!"

Kaylee jumped, startled. Hurriedly she shoved her book under her pillow, shut off the flashlight she had been using, and pulled the blanket back from her face. "Yes, Mom?"

Mom gave her The Look. "You've been reading in bed past your bedtime again, haven't you?"

"Well, I—" Kaylee couldn't actually lie about it. She made a face and sighed.

Mom held out her hand. Frowning, Kaylee pulled out the flashlight and gave it to Mom. Mom took it and held out her other hand. With a great sigh, Kaylee pulled out the book, too.

Mom sat down on the edge of the bed and tucked back the hair that fell across Kaylee's face from being under the blanket. "Listen, Honey, you know I'm not trying to be mean."

"I was only going to read a little bit more," said Kaylee. "I want to know what happens to the lost dog!"

"You can find out tomorrow," said Mom. "This is bad for you in so many ways. First of all, you are growing fast, and must have your sleep. Second, it's hard on your eyes to read that way. The book is too close, the light isn't right, and probably your whole body is in a cramped position, too. Third, you don't get enough oxygen when the blanket is over your head. And fourth, it's important that you learn to wait for things. You're a big enough girl to read some now and some tomorrow. Did you get all your homework done?"

"No..." Kaylee admitted.

"And I can see you didn't clean up your room, as I asked you to. Your new dress that you like so much is crumpled on the floor, your doll's hair will never be the same again if you leave it tossed in the corner like that, you've left food under your bed, and oh, Kaylee, look at your Bible!"

Kaylee looked guiltily at her beautiful white Bible, new last Christmas, which was lying open, upside down, on the floor by her bookshelf.

Mom picked up the Bible and smoothed its pages, sighing. "Kaylee, someday you'll be a grown woman, and you'll have to be responsible. Now is the time to start learning." She leaned forward and kissed Kaylee's forehead. "Did you know stewardship is taking care of God's stuff God's way? And you, my dear, are God's kid! I love you. Now go to sleep."

After Mom left, Kaylee lay there feeling guilty. She knew she could do better, because sometimes she did. Just last week, she'd had her whole room clean, and she'd done her homework and chores every day all week! But then she'd started this new book, and it was really interesting! She guessed she was just lazy.

A week later, Mom said, "Kaylee, I have some exciting news for you! Now that school is out, Aunt Sarah has asked if you'd like to come and stay with her for a whole week!"

Kaylee jumped up and down with joy. A whole week at Aunt Sarah's beautiful apartment in the city! She worked hard that week, cleaning up, packing her things, and making plans. On Sunday, Aunt Sarah came in her blue convertible and they got to ride all the way to the city with the top down and the wind blowing in their hair. It was so cool!

At Aunt Sarah's building, they went up 14 whole floors in an elevator. Aunt Sarah unlocked her door and they walked into the white carpeted room. There were fresh flowers on the coffee table, and the city lights were coming on outside the big window. Aunt Sarah led Kaylee down the hall with her suitcase.

"Here's your room, Kaylee. I hope you like it."

Like it! Kaylee turned around in a circle in the middle of the room. It had wallpaper with pale pink stripes, a huge bed with pink roses on its ruffled bedspread and pink and white satin pillows in the middle, and a fluffy white rug.

"Here's the bathroom," said Aunt Sarah, opening a door.

"My own bathroom?" exclaimed Kaylee. She went into the bathroom, which was as big as her bedroom at home, and it had pearly white bubbles on the shower curtain and a bowl of shells on the sink. The faucets were gold, and there were fluffy towels as big as Kaylee.

"Oh, Aunt Sarah, this is the most beautiful room in the whole world!" she cried, coming back into the bedroom.

Aunt Sarah showed her a crystal bowl on the dresser. "In this dish are some peppermints. They're yours, but you must only have two per day. You may decide when. I'll show you the broom and duster in the hallway, and I expect you to keep your room and bathroom clean. Can you do that for me?"

"Of course!" Kaylee promised.

And she did. Every day, she made her beautiful bed carefully. Sometimes she had to ask Aunt Sarah for help. She wiped around the sink when she brushed her teeth, made sure her hair was out of the bathtub drain, and swept her shiny wood floor every evening.

Aunt Sarah took her out to eat at a fancy restaurant where there were a whole bunch of forks and spoons, and they went to the zoo and to the top of a skyscraper where you could look through a telescope and see all the way across the city.

And every night after supper, Kaylee ate two peppermints. Then she and Aunt Sarah would read one, or maybe two chapters in a really awesome book Aunt Sarah had.

At the end of the week, when Kaylee went back home, Mom said, "Aunt Sarah says you were really responsible this week."

"Yes, Mom, I really was!" said Kaylee.

"Was it hard?"

"No, I liked it!"

"Why do you think that is?" asked Mom.

"Well, everything was so pretty!" said Kaylee.

"Your room is pretty, too, when you keep it nice."

"That's true. But it's not the same." Kaylee thought for a minute, and said, "I think it's because the things weren't mine. Aunt Sarah's house is so beautiful, and I wanted to be sure I didn't hurt anything."

"Good thinking," said Mom. "You were being a good steward."

"I was?"

"Yes, a steward takes good care of things that belong to someone else. I wonder if it would help you to think about your room and your things belonging to God? Would you like taking care of them for Him, the way you took care of Aunt Sarah's things for her?"

Kaylee had to admit, that was a pretty cool thought.

"And how about your health? Did you go to bed on time, and not sneak too much candy?" Kaylee nodded. "Your body belongs to God, too," Mom reminded her. "Why don't you try taking care of His Kaylee His way?"

Kaylee smiled. "I think I will! I'd like to take care of things for Jesus!"

 Thought Question: *Are you taking care of your things and your body as if they belong to Jesus?*

God Made it Grow

You might begin by saying something like, "When God made Adam and Eve, He gave them only one important job to do for Him: take care of the earth and all its plants and animals, and to love and care for each other. Once they disobeyed God, the earth changed, and became much harder to care for. Jesus will soon come back and make a new earth. Now is the time to learn to take care of His earth His way."

This story is suitable for children of any age.

Tom was so excited! It was the day he had been waiting for. Grandpa had promised that they could make a garden together, but then it had rained and rained, and after that Grandpa had been away for several days. After that, they had to wait while Uncle Joe used the big, noisy tiller to dig up the soil until it looked all dark and loose, like Oreo cookies crumbled up. Then the garden had to "rest" a few days. That's what Grandpa said, anyway. Finally, it was a sunny day, and Grandpa was ready.

"Are you ready, Tommy-boy?"

"I'm way ready!" exclaimed Tom.

"Come and help me get things together," said Grandpa.

Together they collected packets of seeds, string, scissors, wooden sticks, a watering can, and two little shovels. They unrolled the hose and laid it out until it reached the edge of the garden.

"First," said Grandpa, "we have to lay out the rows. We'll poke a stick into the ground like this, then we'll tie string to it, and we'll unroll the string all along the garden to the other end."

Tom helped to unwind the string from the ball as they went.

"Then we poke in another stick, right about here" (Tom poked in the stick good and deep so it wouldn't wobble), "and cut off the string and tie it on this stick." Tom tied the string just right.

"That helps us keep our rows straight," said Grandpa. "I like to make wide rows, so we'll plant seeds along both sides of the string. But not yet. First we make more rows."

It seemed to Tommy to take a long time to make all the rows. But it was pretty fun to do. When they were all done, Grandpa said, "Now, we're going to plant the peas on this side of the garden, so they don't shade out the other things. See this wheelbarrow full of branches?"

Tom nodded. "Uncle Joe cut them yesterday. I helped. He said they were called 'pea-sticks.'"

"Exactly," said Grandpa. "We're going to push them into the dirt on both sides of this string. Push them in good and deep, so they stand up strong. When the peas sprout, they'll climb up these sticks."

"They will?" Tom laughed, trying to imagine plants climbing the way he climbed trees.

"Wait and see," said Grandpa.

They got all the pea sticks in, and finally they got to do the part Tom was waiting for. He pushed tiny, shriveled-up, dried peas into the dirt around each pea stick. Then he watered them from the watering can. "Why do we use the can instead of the hose, Grandpa?"

"Because the seeds can be easily washed away. When the plants are big, we'll water with the hose. But right now we'll just use the hose to refill the watering can."

They planted teensy little lettuce and carrot seeds, round, reddish-brown radish seeds, funny-looking, rough spinach and chard seeds, and Tom's favorite—little baby onions! They pushed them right into the dirt with their tiny, little bits of root pointing down and their pointed tops pointing up. "Will these really grow into big onions, Grandpa?"

"Yep," said Grandpa. "Then we'll make onion soup, and salads, and all kinds of good things out of them! We've worked hard today, Tommy-boy. And boy oh boy, my back hurts!"

Tom helped Grandpa up and they watered everything with the watering can. Then they sat on lawn chairs and looked at their garden. "That's a good day's work!" said Grandpa. "Makes me think of the garden of Eden. I'll bet God had a lot of fun planting things for Adam and Eve, and I'll bet they had a lot of fun planting things, too. Even after they disobeyed and things weren't the same anymore, God told them to work in the dirt. It's good for the earth, and it's good for us. We get exercise now, and healthy food later. I think we're being good stewards when we grow some of our own food. We're taking care of God's world God's way."

Every day Tom went out to look at the garden, and every day he saw the same thing—dark, chocolatey-looking dirt. "When's stuff going to grow, Grandpa?"

"Just be patient, Tommy-boy. God will make it grow."

After four days, it rained again. Tom looked out the window sadly, but Grandpa said, "Good! Now we won't have to water again."

After a whole week, Tom went out to look. "Grandpa, Grandpa! Look! Little green stuff!" There were little leaves shaped like hearts where they'd planted the radishes, and pale green ruffles in the lettuce row. Best of all, round green leaves were poking out of the dirt beside the pea sticks. Tom couldn't wait to watch them climb the sticks.

It took a long time, but after that at least it was more interesting. But then there were plants growing that they didn't want—weeds! They had to pull those out and put them on the compost pile. The days got warmer, and they planted beans and corn and pumpkins and little tomato and pepper plants. Tom watched the pea plants put out little, curly tendrils that grabbed hold of the pea sticks and climbed right up. It was cool! They could water with the hose now, but Grandpa was always glad when the rain did it for them.

Finally, the hot summer day came when they got to pick things. Tom was as excited as he'd been clear back in the spring when they started the garden. He carefully helped Grandpa pull some round, red radishes and a couple green onions that had grown tall green leaves, but had not grown big bulbs yet. Then they cut lettuce, spinach, and chard with scissors. "It will grow again and make us more," said Grandpa.

Tom crawled around the pea sticks, finding the fat pods hiding among the leaves and tendrils. They hid really well! "Here's one we missed," said Grandpa.

They took their baskets of food into the kitchen. Tom helped to wash all the dirt off and split the peas out of their pods. "They're just like little green jackets with zippers!" he said, and Grandpa laughed.

They made a salad and put some of the smallest peas in it, raw. They cooked the rest of the peas, and Mom made one of her yummy lentil loaves to go with everything.

At the table, Tom said, "Just think: We made this food ourselves!"

"Well, not exactly," said Grandpa. "We planted it, but God made it grow. He created the earth to provide for us like this. Did you know the Creation story tells about Him making things which grow their seeds inside themselves, like peas? He also intended us to help Him. The first thing He told Adam and Eve was to take good care of the garden and help each other."

"I should have said, God made this food and we helped!" said Tom.

"Right!" said Grandpa.

"And it's going to be yummy!" said Tom.

"Amen!" said Grandpa. "Let's thank Him!"

And they did.

 Thought Question: *How do you think Tom and Grandpa were helping to take care of God's earth and of themselves God's way? Can you help to make a garden this year? If you don't have room, you can grow some things in pots.*

This is My Father's World

You might begin by saying something like, "When God made Adam and Eve, He gave them only one important job to do for Him: take care of the earth and all its plants and animals, and to love and care for each other. Once they disobeyed God, the earth changed, and became much harder to care for. Jesus will soon come back and make a new earth. Now is the time to learn to take care of His earth His way. This is a story about a little girl who wants to help take care of the earth.

This story is suitable for children of any age.

Rosita's Mama and Papa were talking at the table. "They're going to have another clean-up day," said Papa. "Some people will clean up all that trash along the highway, and others will clean up the parks and the riverbanks."

"I wish we could help, but it's always during church time," said Mama.

"Why do people throw trash all over the place, anyway?" asked Rosita.

Mama and Papa both sighed. "I don't know, Chiquita," said Papa. "I guess they don't understand that God made the world for us, to grow food for us, and give us clean water and fresh air, and He asked us to take care of it. Maybe they think the world doesn't matter, or that God doesn't care how we treat it."

"Or they don't know about God at all," said Mama. "They don't seem to understand that when we treat the world badly, we are treating ourselves badly, because that's still where all our food and water comes from, whether we take care of it or not."

"Even the wood for our table and chairs came from the trees," added Rosita. "I wish we could think of a way to help."

"Well, we do help in lots of ways," said Mama. "We don't litter ever, and we keep our own yard clean and take care of our trees, we don't waste water, and things like that."

"Yeah, but I wish we could help when the whole town is cleaning up," said Rosita.

She lay awake for awhile that night, thinking about it, and then she had a great idea! She could hardly wait until breakfast to tell Mama and Papa.

"Mama, Papa!" she said, while everyone was still in robes and Papa hadn't even shaved yet. "I have an idea! Who said we have to wait until the big clean-up day?"

Papa and Mama looked at each other. "Good question," said Mama.

"Wouldn't it be funny if people came to the Memorial Park, the one in the center of town, and it was already cleaned up?" asked Rosita.

Papa and Mama were starting to grin.

"And," said Rosita, "wouldn't it be cool if our whole church worked on it, and left a sign, or something like that? We could all sign it!"

"You're right—that's a great idea!" exclaimed Papa. "I'll call Pastor Will right away!"

The pastor and elders and Sabbath School teachers all loved Rosita's idea, and on the following Sunday, a whole crowd of people from church gathered at Memorial Park. It was a nice park in the middle of town, with some statues, two fountains, and beautiful flower gardens. It didn't look that dirty when they got started, but it was amazing how many garbage bags they filled as they scattered out over the park with bags and gloves. Some people had cool picker-uppers, with little claws on the end, and some used pointed sticks, although most just picked stuff up with gloved hands.

"Eeewww, gross!" said Rosita, dumping old, sticky pop out of a bottle with moss on it. She put it in one of the separate bags they had for plastic bottles and pop cans that would go to the recycling center.

"They'll give us money for the cans," said one of the ladies. "I think we should put that money into Pathfinders, since it was a Pathfinder who thought of this idea!"

"Amen!" said Mrs. Santos, the Pathfinder leader.

There were highways on all sides of Memorial Park, and as the cars circled around, lots of them honked and waved. "They like it that we're cleaning up the park!" said Rosita.

She and the other Sabbath School children had made four big posters, one for each side of the park, and Pastor Will had gotten permission from the city to post them by the gates. They said, "Helping to Take Care of God's World God's Way—your friends the Seventh-day Adventists." They were decorated with flowers, birds, rainbows, and all kinds of bright stuff.

There was a table set up in the middle, by the big statue of a Civil War soldier on a horse. The youth were taking turns at the table when they took breaks from picking up trash. They were giving away free water and flyers about the church. "We go to church on Saturday," they explained to people who stopped by, "so we can't help with the big Clean-up Day next week. But we wanted to do our share."

"That's great!" the people would say, smiling.

After everything was clean, and the bags were loaded into Papa's pickup, everyone washed their hands and gathered by the table.

"Let's sing," said Pastor Will. So they sang "This is My Father's World," and "All Things Bright and Beautiful," and "The Trees are Gently Swaying." They sang all the songs they could think of that talked about God's beautiful world, and some about heaven, too, where nobody would ever throw trash on the ground!

People stopped to listen, and some sang along.

A while later, Rosita was surprised to see a policeman and a woman with a big camera talking to Pastor Will. She went closer to try to hear, but just then Pastor Will turned and clapped his hands loudly to get everyone's attention. "Come, please! Everyone gather over here!"

When everyone got together, Pastor Will said, "This is Police Chief Thomas. He has something to say to us."

Chief Thomas had a loud, booming voice. Nobody had any problem hearing him as he said, "On behalf of the city and of the police department, I'd like to thank you folks for all your hard work today. You've set a good example for all of us that will be working next week!"

Then Pastor Will held out his hand toward the woman with the camera. "This is Helen Gold," he said. "She works for the newspaper, and she wants a picture of all of us for the paper! Rosita, she wants you and your family in the front because it was your idea."

Rosita felt like she was ten feet tall. She'd never been in the newspaper before! Ms. Gold asked some more questions and took a lot of pictures. She even took some photos of Rosita and her friends next to one of the posters they'd made.

And you know what? The next Sabbath, two people came to visit the church that had been in the newspaper for taking care of God's world God's way!

 Thought Question: *How many blessings of God's world can you list that you are thankful for? What are some ways you can take care of God's things God's way?*

Recycle

You might begin by saying something like, "When God made the world and asked Adam and Eve to take care of it, He loaded it with things He knew we would need, especially as the earth got full of more people. We use wood and stone for building, gravel for roads, and oil, gas, and coal for power or heat or gasoline for our cars—all kinds of things! But after sin came into the world, people didn't take good care of these things. God wants us, as Christians, to set the example for others, and take care of God's world God's way. This is a story about two boys and their friends, who are learning about resources."

This story is better suited for school-age children.

Louis and Lincoln were twin brothers. They were in fourth grade at the church school this year, and in science class they were learning a new word: resources.

"Resources," Mr. Kent explained, "are supplies that you need to do things. For example, on the shelves in the back of the room are our supplies of paper, pencils, erasers, and things like that. In the art corner we have paint, big sheets of paper, and big shirts for cover-ups. All of those are resources. Then there are other kinds of resources, like the books in our reading corner, or all the hundreds of books in the library. And on the computer, we can find thousands of other resources. You could say those are resources for our brains. But did you ever think about where those resources come from? Where do we get books?"

Louis raised his hand, and Mr. Kent called on him. "People write them."

"You're right, but what do they write them with?"

"Pens and paper," said Lincoln.

"Computers," said Mary Ann.

"Their brains," said Ella, who liked writing stories herself.

"All true," said Mr. Kent, "but where do they get the paper?"

Hands went up all over the room. "From trees!"

"Pencils, too! They come from trees."

"How about pens, or computers?" asked Mr. Kent.

That was a lot harder. Plastic and metal, they knew that much. "Metal comes from mines," said Johnny. But nobody knew where plastic came from.

"Would you believe petroleum?" asked Mr. Kent. "That's the name for the plain, black oil that comes out of the earth."

Mr. Kent took out some pictures and showed them to the kids.

"This oil is pumped up by big oil derricks, and then it's sent to big buildings where they refine it and get all the impurities out. Some of it makes heating oil for our houses. Some of it makes gasoline for our cars and diesel for trucks. Some of it makes plastic, and believe it or not, some of it makes cloth! That's where polyester and acrylic come from, and that's where some of our paints come from. So here's my question: What happens if we use up all our oil? Everybody look around the room for a minute, and see how much plastic you can find."

The kids found plastic light switches, plastic covers on some of their books, plastic lunch boxes, plastic pencil boxes and key rings, plastic pens, plastic paint brushes, plastic chairs…

"We could go on all day!" said Louis.

"Now imagine that we didn't have any of it," said Mr. Kent.

The kids looked around, their eyes wide. "The room would be half empty," said Lincoln.

"We could make some things out of other stuff," Ella pointed out. "Like metal light switches, and um, we could use pencils instead of pens..."

Johnny liked to read a lot of stories from a long time ago. "They never used to have plastic," he pointed out. "They made stuff out of wood, or glass, or metal. My grandma says she took her lunch to school in a cloth bag."

"So maybe one thing we could do is use less plastic to begin with," suggested Mr. Kent. "Even our toys—that might be where we use the most plastic of all!"

Louis and Lincoln looked at each other. Lincoln loved Lego blocks. He had about a million of them. And come to think of it, they came in plastic buckets, too! Louis had two remote-control cars. Both boys shared a racing car set with plastic cars and a plastic track. Even the housing that held the switches was partly plastic. Maybe the next time they thought of what they wanted for birthdays or Christmas, they could think of things that were made out of wood or cloth. Meanwhile, they could stop leaving the cars lying around where they could get stepped on, and find all the Legos that hid under beds and couches instead of buying more.

"Can anyone think of other things we can do to help keep from running out of oil?" asked Mr. Kent.

"We could take good care of what we have," said Mary Ann. "Like, my Barbie doll's hair is pretty bad, and I was going to ask my mom for a new one. But I bet I could brush it out really, really good, and make her last longer."

"We could drink water out of the faucet," added Johnny. "We don't need all those plastic bottles! Even if you recycle them, my uncle says there are way too many of them. Like billions and billions! He showed me a picture online of an island of garbage in the ocean!"

Louis and Lincoln put their hands up at the exact same second, which made them laugh. "We take cloth bags to the grocery store," said Louis, and Lincoln said, "Hey, I was going to say that!" they both replied, and laughed again.

Mr. Kent turned toward the board and wrote a word: reduce. "Can anyone tell me what that means?"

Lincoln waved his hand. "Use less stuff! Like, do we really need a hundred toys? There are kids that don't have any!"

"Good answer!" said Mr. Kent. He wrote another word: reuse.

Mary Ann raised her hand. "Like what I'm going to do with my Barbie. Keep using her instead of getting another one."

"And if you do have plastic bottles, use them several times before you recycle them," said Johnny.

"And even stuff that isn't plastic, like clothes," added Louis," you can wear them a lot and then when you grow out of them, give them to somebody smaller."

Ella rolled her eyes. "I always have to wear my big sister's stuff!" She sighed. "But I guess I can do that. Mom and I sometimes make some changes, like different buttons, or even dye something a different color."

Mr. Kent wrote his third word: recycle.

All the kids knew that one! "Take it to the recycling place!" exclaimed Johnny, forgetting to raise his hand.

"But that's not all," Louis pointed out. "When Ella wears her sister's stuff, that's like recycling, right? And when Lincoln gets tired of some of his shirts, we trade. That's recycling. In fact, we gave some of our toys to our cousin who is littler than us, and he liked them just as much as if they were new."

"You are all doing some very good thinking," said Mr. Kent. "Now, can anyone tell me what all this has to do with that other big word we are learning: stewardship?"

Hands flew up all over the room.

"The earth is God's."

"The oil is God's."

"The plastic is God's."

"The brains that invented plastic are God's."

Louis summed it all up by saying, "We're God's, and we're taking care of His stuff His way!"

 Thought Question: Are you taking care of God's stuff God's way? How can you do better?

The New Room

You might begin by saying something like, "When God made the world and asked Adam and Eve to take care of it, He loaded it with things He knew people would need, as the earth got full of more people. We use wood and stone for building, and gravel for roads, and oil, gas, and coal for power and heat and gasoline for our cars—all kinds of things! But after sin came into the world, people didn't take good care of these things. God wants us, as Christians, to set the example for others, and take care of God's world God's way. This is a story about some questions one girl has about this subject.

This story is better suited for school-age children.

Donna was sitting by her window, thinking hard.

"You look like you have something on your mind," said her mother.

Donna went over to sit on the couch by Mom. "I have some questions," she announced. "At school, they talk all the time about resources, and reduce, reuse, recycle, and all that stuff. They say our grandkids need to have a good world after we get old and die. In fact, Mrs. Simpkins told us that the way the world will be a million years from now depends partly on us."

Mom sighed. "Well, it's true that the world of tomorrow depends on how we treat the world of today, but this is the issue we have with public school. The teachers aren't considering that we might not still be here on this earth in a million years! I sure wish there was a church school nearby."

"Well, it's okay, Mom." said Donna. "I had a good answer, even though I didn't say it out loud. I thought, yeah, a million years from now we'll be in heaven, and what depends on us is whether we go or not!"

Mom clapped her hands. "Good answer! Even if you didn't say it out loud in class, you might get a good chance to say it to one of your friends."'

"Yeah, but Mom, that's not my question. My question is, since Jesus is coming soon, maybe even before I grow up, then why do we have to worry about whether we run out of stuff like coal or oil?"

"That's a good question," said Mom. "I have two different kinds of answers. Here's one. When I was a little girl like you, I was talking to my grandma, and she was really sad. She said to me, 'I believed Jesus was coming before I grew up. I didn't think I would ever have children of my own. But I did grow up, and I had your mama, and then she grew up and had you, and now, look how fast you're growing up!' I remember being worried. I asked her, 'Do you think Jesus will ever come?' and she said, 'Oh, yes, I know He'll come!' Grandma reminded me of what Jesus said, and I'll bet you can remember it, too, Donna. He said, 'I go to prepare a place for you, and if I go and prepare a place for you...' Then what?"

Donna finished, "'I will come again!' And Jesus never lies, right, Mom?"

"Never!" said Mom. "But I have to admit, grown-ups have been wondering about this very thing for a long time. When is soon?! God has a whole different idea of time than we do, that's for sure!"

"That's because He lives forever," said Donna.

"I think you're right," said Mom. "So that's part of my answer to your question about taking care of the earth. I hope He'll come before you grow up, but you never know! But there's a more important part of the answer. Let's pretend that Dad and I are going to build you a beautiful new room."

"That would be great!" exclaimed Donna. "Could I have a window seat?"

"Let's pretend we're rich and you can have anything you want in your new room. But we're building it as a surprise, so you don't get to see it. We don't even have to ask you for your favorite colors, or anything, because we know you really well, and we know you love blue, and we know you want a window seat, and we know you love four-poster beds and that you need lots of bookshelves, and all that."

"Cool!" said Donna.

"Let's pretend that you know we're building this room, but we're taking a long time about it, or so it seems to you. You can't wait to see it, and sometimes you even wonder if we're really doing it at all! How do you think you'd feel?"

Donna thought about it. "I think sometimes I'd be excited and sometimes I'd be impatient. I'd keep asking you, 'Come on, Mom and Dad, hurry up!'"

"Now," said Mom, "let's pretend you are so excited to get your new room that you stop taking care of the room you have. You don't clean it, and it turns into a pigsty, and there are clothes all over the floor, and window is filthy, and there are so many fingerprints on the light switch that it turns gray, and there's old food under your bed so the whole room stinks, and the bed is never made and never has fresh sheets—"

"Stop, stop!" Donna interrupted, making a face. "Yuck!"

"Let's pretend Dad and I finally finish your new room, and we come to tell you, and we find you in this horrible pigsty. Now how do you think we'd feel?"

"Well, if I were the mom, I wouldn't give a new room to a kid like that!" exclaimed Donna. "She wouldn't deserve it!"

Mom smiled. "Exactly."

Donna thought about that. "Oh, I get it! You mean, why would Jesus want to give a nice, new earth to people who trashed the old one?"

"Well," said Mom, "I believe that our job while we are alive is to try to learn to live the way we want to live in the New Earth. So what are some things you hope will be true about your life in the New Earth?"

"Let me see," said Donna. "I think everybody will be patient and kind, and love everybody all the time, the way God does, so I guess I'd better practice that."

"Excellent. What else?"

"We'll eat perfect food," said Donna. "So I think we should learn to grow and eat good, healthy food here, as much like perfect food as we can. What else, Mom?"

Mom hugged her. "I think we should do our best at things, even things like homework and piano lessons, because our mind is what we're taking with us to heaven, and the kind of workers we are now is the kind of workers we'll be then. And we take care of the things God gives us now, so that—"

"I know!" said Donna. "So we'll be good at taking care of the beautiful things He'll give us then!"

She looked out the window and thought for a while. "And if it takes a long time more, which I hope it doesn't, then the world will still be good for our grandkids because we took care of God's world God's way...right, Mom?"

"Right! But I'm with you—I hope it's a lot sooner than that!"

Donna grinned. "And I'll still watch for a chance to share my other answer with my friends: that a million years from now, the New Earth will be here— so will you be there?"

 Thought Question: Do you want to be there, when Jesus creates the New Earth? What are you doing to help that happen soon, and to take care of God's world God's way, right now?

God's Rooms

You might begin by saying something like, "Stewardship is taking care of God's stuff God's way. One of the most important ways we can do that is to be faithful in serving Him. We can serve God by taking care of people, or taking care of our minds and hearts, or taking care of physical things, and we want to do all of that God's way, because it all belongs to Him. Today's story is about a boy who helps to take care of God's church.

This story is suitable for children of any age.

Michael jumped in the back seat of the car, put down a big bag he'd been carrying, and fastened his seat belt. He was going to Sabbath School, but he wasn't dressed in his church clothes. He was wearing old jeans with a hole in the knee, and a shirt that was too big and had stains all over it. Not only that, it wasn't Sabbath at all—it was Sunday! Michael was excited. "Come on, Mom, hurry up!" he called out his car window.

"I'm coming, be patient!" Mom was wearing old, baggy clothes too, and she was carrying a broom, a mop, a dustpan, and a vacuum cleaner. She put them into the back of the station wagon and got in the driver's seat.

Michael bounced in his seat. "This is going to be cool!"

Mom laughed. "I wish you thought it was cool to clean your own room!" Then she backed out of the driveway and they drove to church. When they pulled into the parking lot, Michael had his seat belt unfastened before the car even stopped. "Hang on, there!" said Mom, turning the car off. "Now you may get out, but don't forget those cleaning supplies, and don't run in the parking lot."

Michael grabbed his bag, which contained a bunch of rags and some bottles and cans of cleaning solution. They were heavy! But he lugged them along as he hurried to the church steps. His friends Jennifer and Marcy were coming up the walk, too. Jennifer carried a bag of cups and a bag of apples and oranges. Marcy was holding a big bowl of potato salad in both hands. Their Grandma was behind them with a tray of sandwiches. Yum! Michael knew that Grandma Curtis made the best bread in the world!

The church door opened and Petey popped his head out. "Hi, guys! Come on, we want to get started!" He held the door for his friends. "Here comes Katrina! What's that you have? More cleaning stuff? We're going to be able to clean a whole village!"

Linda came up the stairs from the basement where the Sabbath School rooms were. "About time you guys all got here!" She turned and led the way as the children trooped down the stairs. "Food goes on the table in the community room," she said to Marcy and Jennifer. "Cleaning supplies come this way!" Linda always knew what everybody should be doing.

Michael and Katrina, and his mom and her dad, hauled all their cleaning things to the Sabbath School room down the hall. "How about a snack before we start?" asked Michael, but Mom just grinned and ruffled his hair.

"Work first, then eat," said Linda in her bossy voice.

"Food first makes us strong enough to work," said Petey.

To their surprise, Mrs. Kinney, who was in the room taking down curtains, agreed. "You're absolutely right, Petey!"

The kids all stared at her, and she smiled at them. "Well, you did have good breakfasts before you came, didn't you?"

They all laughed. "That was hours ago!" said Michael, but he was just kidding. Of course he knew they weren't going to eat anything, not even Mrs. Kinney's oatmeal cookies, until the Sabbath School room was all clean.

"Now that everyone is here, let's pray before we start," said Mrs. Kinney.

Michael was kind of surprised. Pray before work? Like grace at meals?

Mrs. Kinney began by asking, "Why are we here?"

"To clean our Sabbath School room," chorused several people.

"Right!" said Mrs. Kinney. "And...wrong!"

"Wrong?" Michael wrinkled up his face, which always helped him think.

"I get it!" Katrina called out. "We're here to clean up Jesus's Sabbath School room!"

"Give the girl an A!" said her dad.

"So," said Mrs. Kinney, "we are being good..."

She waited. Then the answer came to Michael, "Good stewards!"

"Another A!" said Katrina's dad.

All together the kids chanted, "Stewardship is taking care of God's stuff God's way!"

"Excellent!" said Mrs. Kinney. "Let's pray. Dear God, thank You for all the things You give us. Thank You for our healthy bodies, and for good food, and for our families, and for our church. Thank you for this beautiful Sabbath School room, and help us to take care of it Your way. Amen."

Michael and Linda were the tallest, so they got to wash windows. The stuff they used made Michael sneeze, but he polished until the windows shone.

Katrina and Jennifer took all the books out of the shelves, dusted them, dusted the shelves, and put them all back. They sorted out the old books nobody read anymore, so they could give them away.

Petey, his mom, and Marcy organized all the craft stuff and threw away a bunch of junk. "Why is this stuff even here?" demanded Marcy, holding up a long coil of tangled yarn.

Katrina's dad and Michael's mom pulled the furniture to one side of the room, rolled up the rug, and hauled it outside, where they hung it up and beat a cloud of dust out of it, then left it in the sunshine while they swept the floor.

"Are we ready to mop yet?" asked Michael's mom.

"Almost. I have to get the rest of these songbooks put back," said Jennifer.

Michael was really hungry now. "I have an idea!" he announced. "Since we all have to get out while you mop, anyway, how about if we eat lunch while it dries?"

"Exactly what I was going to suggest," said Mom. "You may go and help arrange the table and get the food out while we mop. It will only take a few minutes. When we're through, we'll come and say the blessing and eat together."

So everybody who wasn't mopping washed up (the water was dirty!) and went to set up the meal.

When they had gathered together, all clean and hungry, Michael said, "This is really fun! Maybe it would be more fun to clean our rooms if we did them together!"

"Hey, maybe it would!" said Jennifer.

"I bet it would really help if we thought of our rooms as God's rooms, just like the Sabbath School room is God's room," said Linda.

And nobody even minded that she was using her bossy voice. She was right!

 Thought Question: *What is a way that you can serve God and take care of His things His way?*

God's Faithful Servant

You might begin by saying something like, "Stewardship is taking care of God's stuff God's way. One of the most important ways we can do that is to be faithful in serving Him. We can serve God by taking care of people, or taking care of our minds and hearts, or taking care of physical things; and we want to do all of that God's way, because it all belongs to Him. Today's story is about a girl who wants to serve God."

This story is suitable for children of any age.

Shayna was bored. She wriggled on the hard pew. She had already filled the back of Dad's bulletin with doodles, and made lots and lots of little marks under the words Love, God, Jesus, and Grace that Mom had assigned for her to do. She counted the marks. Pastor Jenson had said God 27 times, Jesus 13 times, Love 33 times, and Grace 18 times. He might say some of them again, but she was tired of listening.

Oh, good!, Shayna thought. Finally, there goes the organ.

Dad and Mom were finding their place in the hymnal and standing up to sing. Shayna stood too, and Mom held her hymnal where Shayna could see it: "The Old, Rugged Cross." Good, she knew the chorus of that one. She followed the words with her finger as she sang along.

On the way home in the car, Mom said, "Shayna, you really are getting big enough to not wiggle around so much during the church service. Did you listen at all to the sermon?"

"Sure, I listened. He said God 27 times."

"That's not what I meant," said Mom.

But before she could say anymore, Shayna asked, "Mom, why do we call it a church service?"

"That's a good question, Shayna," said Dad. "Do you know what service means?"

Shayna thought about it. "It seems like it means all kinds of stuff. Aunt Jodie says Bo is 'in the service,' and she means the army. I heard Grandpa say that the restaurant had 'bad service,' and you say 'service' for church, too. What does it mean, Daddy?"

Dad and Mom laughed a little in the front seat. "I guess it is a little confusing, with all that, but it's really quite simple. It comes from 'to serve,' which means to wait on someone, like a servant." Dad was starting to use his school teacher voice. "Most people don't have servants anymore, but my mama, your grandma, used to clean people's houses for them. That's one kind of service. When we go to a restaurant, the people who bring our food are called 'servers,' because what they do is serve us."

"So they're helpers, kind of," said Shayna.

"Right. And in the army, Bo is serving his country, helping to protect it. Any kind of helping or taking care of somebody is service. It's really important, too, because we're all God's servants, and the most important thing we can do is serve Him. Most of the time, we serve God by serving other people. When Grandma used to clean houses, she tried to think of it as cleaning for Jesus. When mamas and daddies take care of their children, they try to remember they're doing it for God, because children really belong to God. Then there are some people who give their whole lives to serve God in special ways, like pastors and teachers. And that's why we call church a service, because the pastor and elders and teachers are all serving God."

"But we're all serving God during church, too," added Mom. "We're serving God directly, when we sing to Him or when we give money for His work, and we're also coming to church to get trained, you could say—to listen to the sermon and our Sabbath School lessons and learn more about how to serve God all week long."

"So what did you learn today about serving God?" asked Dad.

Shayna tried to remember what they'd talked about in Sabbath School. "Ms. Singer said that stewardship is taking care of God's stuff God's way. She said all our things and our houses and toys and even us—everything belongs to God, and we're just taking care of it. So does that mean when we take care of God's stuff, we're serving Him?"

"That's exactly what it means."

"Well, then," said Shayna, "I think it would be a lot more fun if I could really do something to serve God at church instead of just sitting still!"

Daddy and Mom looked at each other. "That's a good idea, Shayna. What kinds of things would you like to do?"

Shayna thought again. She couldn't exactly preach a sermon! And she didn't know how to play the organ. "I could pass out bulletins," she said. "And I bet I could help lead songs, or maybe take up offerings. And, what else? I know! I could greet people and say 'Happy Sabbath.' And if I practiced, I think I could read a Bible verse sometimes."

"Well, I think you've really hit on some good ideas!" said Mom. "I'll talk to Pastor Jenkins and to Elder Simon about it. Maybe you and the other kids could help in church sometimes."

Shayna gave a little bounce in her seat. Maybe church was about to get a lot less boring!

The next Sabbath, Shayna got to stand at the door with Mrs. Jenkins and Mrs. Simon, greeting people and giving them a bulletin. Two of her friends from Sabbath School got to help take up the offering with the grown-ups (they had to wait until they were a little bit older to do it alone).

But the truly surprising thing was, after the sermon had started, Shayna forgot to mark down the times Pastor Jenkins said God. She was listening for ways she might be able to serve. Pastor Jenkins was talking about the little girl who was taken far away from her home to be a servant to Namaan and his wife in Syria.

For the first time, Shayna realized that little girl, maybe not much older than herself, learned to serve in two ways. She worked for Namaan and his wife every day, doing ordinary household things like washing dishes, maybe, or sweeping floors, and she also served them and God by telling Namaan about God and about the prophet Elisha. Because of her, a great army general was healed of leprosy!

"This little girl, even though she was a child," said Pastor Jenkins, "was a faithful servant of God."

Shayna wanted to be a faithful servant of God, too. She found out there were lots of ways she could do that. She could do her best in school, and help with housework, and do her chores without fussing. She could take care of her money, and not eat junk food, and put plastic and glass in the recycling bin.

She could even share with her friends. One of them asked her, "Do you have to go to church every week? That must be so boring!"

"It used to be," said Shayna, "but not anymore. Now I'm learning to be God's faithful servant."

"You are?"

"Yeah! I'm taking care of God's stuff God's way!"

"What's God's stuff?" asked her friend.

Shayna grinned. "Everything!" she exclaimed, whirling in a circle with her arms out. "Every single thing! Even you! Come eat lunch with me, and I'll tell you all about it!"

 Thought Question: *Are you a faithful servant of God, taking care of His stuff His way?*

You're Hired!

You might begin by saying something like, "Stewardship is taking care of God's stuff God's way, and the one thing that's more important to God than any other thing in the whole universe is His children. When we serve God by giving faithful service to our fellow human beings, everyone is blessed. Today's story is about a boy who wants to take care of God's kids God's way."

This story is about an older child, but may still be enjoyed by younger kids as there are younger characters in the story.

Anthony needed to make some money. His ancient, thrift-store bike was getting harder to fix each time. He really needed a new one, or at least a newer one, so Anthony was doing every odd job he could find. He cleaned the garage for his dad, raked the lawn for Mr. Brenner, weeded Mrs. James' flower beds, and took a package to the post office for Mrs. King, carrying it in the basket of his old, rickety bike. He'd even picked up all the aluminum cans within a mile (or so it seemed) of his house and turned them in at the recycling center.

So far he'd been working for four whole weeks, and all he had was $38! At this rate, he would be old and gray before he earned enough for a whole new bike!

Then one evening, his mom told his dad, "Joan's taking a six-week online course for her home business. She did the first session last night, but the boys interrupted her so much that she wants a babysitter, just to keep them out of her hair for two hours. It's too bad I can't do it. The webinars are exactly the time I'm helping with choir rehearsals for the special church program. I wouldn't charge her, of course, but she says she'll pay $5 per hour."

Ten dollars every week, for six weeks. Anthony was on it! "Mom, I could do it!" he said.

"You?" Mom said, looking surprised, and also like she was about to say "No."

Anthony hurried on. "She lives right next door, she'll be there in the house, I can do it, Mom!"

"What if you have to change Calvin's diaper?" asked Dad.

"I can do that, too. Aunt Joan taught me, back when he was tiny."

"Yes, but Anthony, it's a lot harder to put a diaper on a squirming one-year-old baby! I really think…"

"Oh, please, Mom! You know I'm trying to save money! Let me try it just once, and then if Aunt Joan isn't satisfied, she can get somebody else! Please?"

Mom and Dad agreed, as well as Aunt Joan, and a week later, Anthony found himself in a messy playroom with one-year-old Calvin, three-year-old Josiah, and four-year-old Martin.

"Okay, guys, this is going to be fun!" Anthony promised, getting down on his knees and starting a tower of building blocks. It was fun—for about 20 minutes. Then Calvin started crying for Mama, and Martin hit Josiah over the head with a toy truck, and the rain, which had already kept them inside, turned into a loud thunderstorm.

Anthony took the truck away from Martin and made him say "sorry" to his brother. He picked Calvin up, checked his diaper, and jounced him around the room until he started giggling. Then Martin and Josiah had to be jounced around, too. And then Calvin did need a change, and Josiah had to have help to go potty. By the time the two hours were over, Anthony was TIRED! He thought it might be easier to clean out ten garages! But when Aunt Joan gave him $10, a hug, and a big thank you, he decided it was worth it.

The second week it was sunny, and they played outside. That was better. The third week, all three boys were sleepy, so Anthony read them a story and they all fell asleep on the rug. That was great! He looked at the three tousled little heads and smiled. They were hard work, but they were cute little guys. And the story he read reminded him that they were also Jesus' little lambs. Anthony quietly sang "Jesus Loves Me," even though they were out like lights and couldn't hear him.

He felt kind of guilty for taking money that day, but Aunt Joan said he was worth a million bucks and she wished she could give him that much. Anthony laughed, thanked her, and went home to count his money. He'd found four more small jobs, and now he had almost $90. The bike he had his eye on was $120. He figured he'd need at least $20 extra in order to give back God's ten percent tithe, plus some to give for offering. That made $140. Only $50 to go!

The fourth week, disaster struck.

The four boys were out in the backyard. Josiah and Martin were making truck noises in the sand box, and Calvin was crawling around the grass, inspecting clover blossoms. Anthony now had well over $100, and he was looking at a bicycle magazine he'd brought—and he wasn't paying enough attention. Calvin had just started taking some steps lately. He decided now was a good time to try out his new skill, and he managed to push himself up on the wooden edge of the sandbox. He toddled three steps, then fell over sideways.

Anthony was jerked out of his magazine-reading by a shriek. He looked up and saw the screaming baby, lying on the ground by the sandbox, with blood pouring from a cut in his head. Anthony raced over to pick him up. Both of the older boys were starting to cry, too.

The screen door banged open and Aunt Joan ran into the yard. "Oh, my word!" she cried, grabbing her baby. "What happened?"

"I—I'm not sure," stammered Anthony.

"He fell and hit his head on the board," whimpered Martin, pointing to the edge of the sandbox.

"Bring them in—hurry!" Aunt Joan dashed in the house with a crying, bleeding Baby Calvin.

Anthony didn't have to get the others. They climbed out of the sandbox and ran after their mother, wailing.

It was a confusing half hour. The next door neighbor on the other side heard the commotion and came over. She was a nurse, and her calmness made everyone feel better. "Of course, you can call an ambulance if you want to, Joan, but you don't really need to. Head wounds always bleed a lot. Let's clean it up and see what we've got."

The cut really wasn't that big, and it was soon bandaged with a funny kind of bandage called a "butterfly." Calvin was distracted with a snack, and the two older boys settled down when he did, and begged for snacks too. Anthony got them something to nibble on, but as for himself, he felt sick to his stomach.

When Aunt Joan finally had time to talk to him, he said bravely, "It was my fault, Aunt Joan. I was looking at a picture of the kind of bike I want, and I wasn't watching. I'm really sorry!" He took a deep breath. "I'll give you back the money you've paid me so far and you can get a better babysitter."

Aunt Joan put her arm around his shoulders. "That's not necessary, Anthony. This is the kind of thing that can happen to anybody. Did you know that Martin once broke his arm because I wasn't paying close attention? The question is, what have you learned? What will you do differently?"

Anthony had been thinking about that very thing while the bandaging was going on. "I was taking care of them just because I wanted the money," he confessed. "If you trust me again, I want to take care of them because they're Jesus' little lambs."

Aunt Joan hugged him. "Great answer! You're hired!"

Anthony felt a lump in his throat. "Thanks, Aunt Joan. From now on, I'll leave the magazines at home and take care of God's kids God's way!"

 Thought Question: *What are some ways you can serve God's other children?*

God's Kids

You might begin by saying something like, "Stewardship is taking care of God's stuff God's way, and the one thing that's more important to God than any other thing in the whole universe is His children. When we serve God by giving faithful service to our fellow human beings, everybody is blessed. Today's story is about a girl who wants to take care of God's kids (even grown-ups!) God's way.

This story is suitable for children of any age.

"Mom, is it true that you're God's kid, even if you are old?" asked Lisa.

Mom laughed. "Well, I might seem old to you, but you know, God lives forever! To Him I'm practically a baby! And yes, I'm His kid. Why do you ask?"

"Well, Miss Gina was saying that one way to be a good steward—wait, do you know what a steward is, Mom?"

"I think so, but why don't you tell me, just in case I've forgotten?"

"Stewardship is taking care of God's stuff God's way. And Miss Gina was saying that one way to do that is to take care of God's other kids—which means everybody. Like, she said that even if you just smile at the lady who checks us out at the store, that's being kind, and it might help that lady. Maybe she's having a bad day, or she's tired, and you don't even know it, but your smile makes her happier."

"I think Miss Gina is exactly right," said Mom.

"Well, I want to take care of God's kids God's way," said Lisa. "And I think I have an idea, but I want to keep it a secret right now. May I go outside of our yard if I only go to the corner?"

"Yes, you may," said Mom. "Are you going to tell me your secret later?"

"Yep! I'll tell you and Daddy both at supper."

Lisa skipped out the door, smiling. She was pretty sure her idea was a really good one.

She walked to the house next door, where Mr. Barney lived. He was a funny old man, and sometimes grouchy, but Lisa thought maybe he was tired or had a bad day, like Miss Gina said. She rang Mr. Barney's doorbell.

The door opened. Mr. Barney looked like he hadn't combed his hair that day. "Yeah, what do you want?" he asked grumpily.

"Hi, Mr. Barney, did you know you're one of God's kids? Even though you're old, to God you're practically a baby!" said Lisa.

Mr. Barney's bushy eyebrows went almost up to his hairline. "Huh?"

"I want to take care of God's kids God's way," Lisa explained. "Is there something I can do for you?"

Mr. Barney scratched his head. It took him a minute to understand what Lisa meant, but finally he said she could take the broom on his porch and sweep the leaves off his walkway. While she was at it, Lisa took two newspapers that Mr. Barney hadn't yet picked up and put them on the porch.

When she left, she could see him looking through his curtains at her. Lisa waved.

The next house was Mrs. Waverly's house. She was really nice and had two cats that Lisa sometimes played with. "Hi, Mrs. Waverly, did you know you're one of God's kids?" Lisa asked.

Mrs. Waverly smiled. "I certainly am! And so are you!"

"Well, I want to help take care of God's kids God's way. Is there anything I can do for you today?"

"Well, how sweet, dear! As a matter of fact, I was just wishing I had someone to help me get these garbage bags into the big trash can, and wheel the can down to the curb. Do you think you could help me do that?"

Of course Lisa could help with that, and she did. The Carters weren't home at the next house, but Lisa saw that the little kids' toys were all over the yard, so she picked them all up and took them to the porch. She smiled to herself when she imagined their surprise. Doing things secretly was even more fun!

There was only one more house before the corner, and Lisa had promised not to go farther than that. She knocked on the door of the house and waited for Aunt Louise to answer. Aunt Louise wasn't really anybody's aunt, but that's what everybody in the whole neighborhood called her.

The door opened slowly, and Aunt Louise looked out. She smiled at Lisa, but Lisa thought her eyes looked kind of red. "Are you sick, Aunt Louise?" she asked.

"No, honey, I'm not sick. I'm kind of busy, though, so what do you need?"

"Maybe I can help, if you're busy," said Lisa. "I'm going around finding ways to help take care of God's kids God's way. Did you know you're one of God's kids?"

To Lisa's surprise, Aunt Louise started to cry! She put a wadded up tissue to her face.

"What's the matter, Aunt Louise? Do you want me to get my mom?"

Aunt Louise sniffed and wiped her eyes. "No, I don't need your mom, but thank you. Tell you what—why don't you sit down here on the porch swing with me for a while. Do you have time to do that?"

"Of course," said Lisa.

She and Aunt Louise sat on the bench seat of the porch swing and Lisa rocked them slowly back and forth with her feet.

"Now, then, dear, tell me why you think I'm one of God's kids," said Aunt Louise, crumpling her tissue the way Lisa did sometimes, when she was upset.

"Oh, I know you are! Everybody is!" Lisa said eagerly. "Even when we're really old, God lives forever, so we seem like little babies to Him. He loves us all, and He wants us to take care of each other! That's what I'm doing today. Mom said I could go to the corner, so you're my last house. If you're really busy, I could help you." She looked up at Aunt Louise's sad face.

"Well," said Aunt Louise slowly, "I'm not really busy. I just didn't want to tell you I felt so sad and lonely today. Did you know that there are some days when grown-ups don't feel like they are God's kids?"

Lisa shook her head. "No, I didn't know that. Why?"

"Well, you know, sometimes we do things we wish we hadn't done, or say things we wish we hadn't said."

"Oh, you mean bad things?" Lisa asked. "I do bad things sometimes, but my mommy and daddy still love me. I'm still their kid. You just have to say you're sorry, that's all."

Aunt Louise was crying again, but she was smiling, too. "What do your mommy and daddy do when you say you're sorry?"

"They hug me real tight and tell me they love me!" said Lisa. "And I promise not to do it again."

Aunt Louise gave a big sigh. Then she turned toward Lisa. "Well, in that case, I know just how you can help me. You know, since Jesus went back to heaven, the only way He can hug us is through other people. Do you think you could give me a big hug?"

Lisa gave her a really tight hug. Then she said, "Just tell God and the other person you're sorry. And promise not to do it again."

"I will," promised Aunt Louise. "And thank you so much, Lisa. You've done a wonderful job of taking care of God's kids today!"

"Are you sure there's nothing else I can do for you?"

"No, nothing right now. It's getting close to supper time. You'd better go home now. Tell your mother I'll call her, okay?"

"Okay!" Lisa skipped toward home. She would have lots of good stories to tell Mom and Dad tonight!

 Thought Question: How can you help take care of God's kids God's way? Remember not to do what Lisa did unless you know all the people you go to, as she did.

God's Money

You might begin by saying something like, "One of the simplest things we can do to take care of God's stuff God's way is tithing. God gives us strength and intelligence to earn money, and He says ten percent of it is His. Here is a story about a boy who is learning about tithe."

This story is a simple explanation of tithe and money management, and is best for young children. Have them hold up their own hands and figure tithe when Randall does in the story.

"Happy birthday to you, happy birthday to you, happy birthday, dear Randall, happy birthday to you!"

Randall clapped his hands as all his friends, plus Mom, Dad, and his big sister, Sandy, sang to him. He was six years old today! He would be going to first grade soon!

The day after his birthday, Dad sat down on the couch with him and said, "Randall, I have some good news for you. Mom and I have decided that you are big enough to get an allowance now."

"Oh, yay!" exclaimed Randall. He had wished for a long time that he could get money of his own every week, just like Sandy. He would be able to buy his own stuff! "How much?" he asked Dad.

Dad smiled. "We've decided that five dollars a week is a good place to start— but before we do that, we have to talk about some things. You remember what stewardship is, right?"

"Yeah! Stewardship is taking care of God's stuff God's way!" Randall answered.

Dad held out a nice, new, five-dollar bill. "So who does this money belong to?"

Randall hesitated. It was Dad's, right now. But when Dad gave it to Randall, it would be his, right? He looked up at Dad. "Is it still God's, even when it's mine?"

"Yes, because you are God's boy, remember? Every single thing belongs to God, even this house and this couch. And definitely this money!"

Randall was confused. "Yeah, but how is it mine if it's God's?"

"Here's how it works," said Dad. "God made the world, and He made the people. He asked the people to take care of the world, and He gives each person certain things to take care of. All God's children are supposed to take care of each other, too. He even wants you and Sandy to help take care of each other, and to help Mom and me."

"Like when I helped you do the dishes last night," said Randall.

"Exactly," Dad answered. "So one of the things God gives us is work, and when you're old enough, you'll have a job like mine, where the people give you money for doing your work. The money itself isn't what's important. You use the money for taking care of the people and things God has given you to take care of. All of that is part of what we call stewardship. So Mom and I want you to start now, learning to take care of a little bit of money God's way, so it will be easier when you're grown up."

Randall nodded. He liked the feeling that he was learning to do a grown-up thing when he took good care of his allowance.

"But," said Dad, and Randall could tell by his voice that something important was coming. "Do you remember what the very first you do with your new earnings?"

Randall bounced on the couch. "I remember! Tithe!"

Dad gave him a high five. "I knew you would remember! Since it's God's money, He gets His share first. Do you remember how much that is?"

Randall wrinkled his eyebrows, thinking. "I remember that if you have ten dimes, one dime belongs to Jesus."

"Do you remember how many dimes are in a dollar?"

"Yep—ten!"

"Excellent!" said Dad. He held up the five-dollar bill again. "But we can't cut this bill in ten pieces, can we?"

Randall laughed. "No!"

"Right. So here's what we'll do. Hold up your five fingers."

Randall did.

"We'll pretend each finger is one dollar—1, 2, 3, 4, 5. That means each finger represents ten dimes, right?"

Randall looked at his hand and thought about it. "Yeah, I get it."

"Good. So for each finger, how many dimes belong to God?"

"One."

"And how many dimes does God get out of all five?"

Randall counted out the dimes on his fingers. "Five!"

"Right! The tithe on five dollars is five dimes, which is 50 cents."

"That's not very much for God, Dad. Why doesn't He take half of it, or something?"

"Good question! I think the way God thinks about it is if you take care of all His money His way, then in one way or another, it all goes back to Him. God loves you, right? So when I use some of the money God gives me to buy you food and clothes, that makes God happy, too, right?"

"Yeah, I guess so. So God gets 50 cents and then I get the rest to spend?"

"Well, you might want to give an offering, too. God's share is already His. Do you want to give Him any more than that?"

"Yeah, I want to give Him another 50 cents."

"That makes it easy," said Dad. "That means one dollar of your five goes to church, where they collect the money for God's work, such as telling people about Him. Then you get to spend the rest, but remember, I want you to learn to use it wisely. So it doesn't all go to candy, right?"

"I'd get sick on that much candy!" said Randall.

"Good thinking," said Dad. "Now hold out your hand." Randall did, and Dad laid the five-dollar bill in it. "We'll go to the store later. We can get change and you can take out your tithe and offering. Then we'll see what kinds of things you might want to do with your share of the money. And we'll talk and learn more and more about money as you grow up, okay?"

"Okay! Thanks, Dad!" Randall hugged Dad. He felt really grown up, with his own five dollars in his hand. Maybe he'd buy some presents for Mom, Dad, and Sandy with it!

 Thought Question: *Do you have money of your own to manage for God? Are you faithful to give God's share back to Him?*

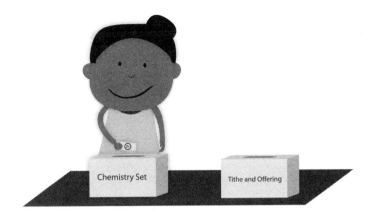

The Chemistry Kit

You might begin by saying something like, "One of the simplest things we can do to take care of God's stuff God's way is tithing. God gives us strength and intelligence to earn money, and He says ten percent of it is His. Here is a story about a girl who is learning about tithe."

This story is a more complex explanation of tithe and money management, and is best for school-age children. You may want to have a white board or paper to show the math that Andrea and her dad work out.

Andrea skipped in through the kitchen door yelling, "Dad, are you here? Where are you?"

Dad called from the living room, "In here, Andrea!"

Andrea went to the living room, where her dad was coiling up the vacuum cleaner cord. The carpet had neat, diagonal stripes on it from the vacuum.

Andrea waved a handful of dollar bills. "Dad, I might have enough for my chemistry kit, but I can't figure out the tithe! I need help."

Andrea had been doing yard work for the neighbors for weeks and weeks, saving and counting her money. The chemistry kit was pretty expensive, but Andrea really wanted one. She was thinking about being a scientist someday.

Dad turned from the vacuum cleaner. "Well, you know how to figure ten percent, right?"

"Yeah, but here's the mistake I made. The chemistry kit is $130. I knew I needed ten percent extra for tithe, and ten percent of $130 is $13, right?"

"Right."

"So I saved up $143, but that makes the tithe $14.30, and that leaves only $128.70! It's confusing, Dad! Plus, I want to be able to give some offering, too."

"You've also forgotten some details," Dad told her. "There will be tax on the kit, plus shipping. Have you looked to find out how much that is?"

Andrea sighed and rolled her eyes. "This is too hard!"

"No, it's not, it just takes some time and some thinking," said Dad. "That's what stewarding our money is all about: thinking and planning ahead. That's why Mom and I want you to learn this now, because if you think this is complicated, wait until you have to do a whole household budget!"

Andrea knew that a budget was the paper her parents made out every month, listing all the bills and gas for the car, and what she needed for school, and everything. Dad had told her he would help her make a simple budget for her allowance, but right now, all her money was being saved for just one thing—the chemistry set.

Then Dad said, "You know, what you're trying to figure out now is almost like a simple budget. Here's some paper. I'll help you make a list."

Under Dad's guidance, Andrea wrote down $130 for the price of the chemistry set. They looked up the tax, which was $7.80. She wrote that down. Shipping was another $14, which made her yelp, but Dad pointed out that they had to pack the set carefully so it wouldn't break on its way to their house.

Andrea added up what she had so far. "$151.80!" she exclaimed. "And that's not even with tithe and offering! How much more do I need?"

"What I do is add an extra chunk of money to the total—more than I think I'll need. In this case, about $30," said Dad. "Then, I can subtract God's tithe, plus any offering I want to give, and still have some left over after I buy the thing I'm saving for. Why don't you figure out how much you'd have if you had $180?"

Andrea wrote down $180. Tithe on that was $18, which left $162. She could give $10 offering, and still have $152, just a bit more than she needed for her chemistry set.

"Thanks for helping me figure it out, Dad, but boy, I sure have a lot more work to do! I still need almost $40 more!"

"Work is good for…" Dad began, and Andrea laughed and said, "I know, I know, work is good for the character! Well, I should have a pretty good character, then!"

Dad hugged her. "You do have a good character. I'm proud of you."

"Thanks, Dad. Do you have any work you want me to do?"

Dad grinned. "I do, but it's not paying work, I'm afraid. I need you to help me get supper ready tonight. Mom has to work late."

Andrea was thoughtful as she helped to get the meal ready, and after they asked God to bless the food, Dad asked Andrea what she was thinking about.

"Well, I was thinking about how stewardship is taking care of God's stuff God's way. Is getting a chemistry set doing God's stuff God's way?"

"Good question," said Dad. "Why do you want the chemistry set?"

"Because I want to be a scientist."

"And why do you want to be a scientist?"

"I don't know, I just like science."

"You know not everybody likes science, right?"

Yes, Andrea knew that. Some of her friends thought she was weird for liking "boring old science."

"So," asked Dad, "Who do you suppose created your brain and gave you an interest in the natural world?"

"God…but why didn't He make Lora like it, then?"

"He created Lora to like music instead."

"Oh, I see. He likes people to be different." Andrea thought some more. "So, if I grow up and use science to make life better for people, will I be doing God's will?"

"Honey, all service to human beings is doing God's will. I'm doing God's will when I deliver the mail from house to house. Mom is doing it when she takes care of sick people in the hospital. We all are doing it when we keep our house clean and take care of each other. It's not what you do, it's how you do it."

Just then, Mom came home from work, looking tired from a 12-hour shift. Andrea hugged her and gave her the supper they'd saved for her. "Thank you, you two!" Mom said with a smile. "Now before I forget, Andrea, Grandpa gave me a letter for you."

Andrea opened the envelope Mom handed her, and something fell out. When she bent down to pick it up, it was a check! "Hey, look, Grandpa sent me $20! I wonder why?" She read her letter. "Listen to this, Mom and Dad, Grandpa says he heard I was saving up for a chemistry set, and he wants to help! Isn't that nice of him? He says he wants to have a famous scientist in the family." She laughed. "I don't know if I'll get famous, but I'll try to be a good one!"

She turned to take her money upstairs to her room, and then turned back. "Wait—do you tithe gifts, too?"

"God says to tithe all our increase," said Mom. "Do you know what increase is?"

"It's everything we get, right? Then I guess you do tithe it. It sure increases the amount I have now, and decreases the amount I still have to earn. I think I'll call Grandpa on the phone and tell him thank you!"

And she did!

 Thought Question*: Are you learning to manage money God's way? If you want to learn more about it, ask a grown-up you trust.*

The Lamb's Offering

You might begin by saying something like, "You remember, don't you, that ten percent of our money (which is all really God's money anyway) is returned to Him as tithe? After we've done that, we can choose to give an offering. Here is a story about some children who want to give God an offering."

This story is suitable for children of any age.

When the piano started to play "Jesus Loves Me," the children knew it was story time before the elder even announced it. They hurried up to the front pew of the church, but of course, they didn't run!

They excitedly filled the front pew. Mary squeezed in next to Margie, and Andy and Mark made sure they were by Tim. They politely made room for the visiting kids.

"It's Miss Tina!" Margie whispered to one of the visitors. "Her stories are the best!"

And sure enough, Miss Tina told the children a really cool story about some kids in India that were helping their mom make enough money to buy food and clothes for the whole family.

Then came one of their other favorite parts—the Lambs' Offering. The kids hurried to get baskets, and made sure the visiting children got one each. Then they moved out through the congregation, collecting lots of change and a few dollar bills. Mark even got a five-dollar bill! The children all took the baskets back to the front and Miss Tina helped them line them up on the edge of the platform. Then they went back to their seats to listen to the sermon.

After church, while their parents were still talking, the kids gathered in the hallway outside their Sabbath School rooms. One of the visitors, a boy named Mikey, asked, "Why do the kids collect money?"

Mary explained, "The Lambs' Offering is always for children. Sometimes it's for Adventurers and Pathfinders, some really cool clubs we have. If you move here, you can join. Right now we're saving up to have a super awesome Vacation Bible School! You should definitely come to that if you're here this summer!"

Mikey's big sister, Anna, asked, "If it's a special offering for kids, why don't kids give to it?"

All the kids looked at each other. "I don't know," said Andy. "That's a good idea!"

"But we already gave our tithe," Tim objected.

"What's tithe?" asked Mikey.

Mary explained again. "Tithe is ten percent of all our money and stuff. It all belongs to God anyway, you know—even you belong to God, because He made you. So all our money is His, too, and we're supposed to take care of it, because stewardship—" (all the kids chimed in together) "is taking care of God's stuff God's way!" They all laughed, and Mary continued. "But God asks us to give Him back ten percent of it, which is called tithe, as His share, for His work in the world, like telling people Jesus loves them."

She turned to Tim. "So we didn't give our tithe. We gave it back, or returned it. It was God's already."

"Yeah," said Margie. "If we kept that, we'd be stealing! And stealing is always bad, but stealing from God is really bad!"

Anna and Mikey looked confused. "But how do you know all this?"

"It's in the Bible! We'll show you!"

"Wait—what's an offering, then?"

This time Mark explained. "Offering is what you give to God after you give Him back His tithe, however much you want to give, because He loves a cheerful giver. That's in the Bible, too."

Anna shook her head. "We'll have to learn all about this, but I still want to know—if the Lambs' Offering is for kids, why don't we give to it?"

Mary looked around the group. "Well, why don't we, then?" she asked, and all the kids said, "Yeah, let's!"

"But," added Mary, "not our Sabbath School mission offering. We still need that to tell kids all around the world about Jesus. Let's find a way to give some extra to the Lambs' Offering."

That week, when Mary and Tim got their allowances, they took out God's ten percent, then the amount they liked to give to Sabbath School mission offering, and then they took out another offering for this year's Vacation Bible School.

"It's not very much," said Tim.

"That's okay," said Mary. "When we put it together with everybody else's, God can use it for great stuff. I once heard that if every person in the world, even the grown-ups, just gave one quarter, it would be, like, billions of dollars!"

"Cool!" said Tim.

Margie, Andy, and Mark didn't have allowances, so they asked their parents and neighbors if they could do some jobs and earn some. Andy weeded his mom's flower beds and got $7. Mark helped his dad wash the car and got $5. Margie helped her aunt do a lot of dishes after a big party and got $10! They took out their tithe, their Sabbath School mission offering, and some extra for the Lambs' Offering.

Anna and Mikey told their mom, "We loved that church! Can we go again?"

"I think we will," said Mom. "I liked it too!"

They didn't get an allowance and knew their mom couldn't afford to pay them to help her, but they had some special savings their grandparents had given them for birthdays. They were a little unsure about this new idea of tithe, but they sure didn't want to rob God! So they took out ten percent, and then some extra for the Lambs' Offering. After all, they hoped to be going to the VBS, so they would like to help with it!

The following Sabbath, when the children all gathered for story time, they seemed a little more giggly and wiggly than usual. Uncle Joe, who was going to tell the story, said, "Hey, guys, settle down." So they did, but they could hardly wait for Lambs' Offering.

Still, Uncle Joe's story was really great, and it captured their attention. It was from when he was a little boy, which was a really long time ago, because Uncle Joe was pretty old. He had actually had to help cut wood for his family's wood stove!

After the offering, they hurried to get baskets. Grinning at each other, because they'd planned this all out, they fanned out through the congregation and collected lots of change and a few dollar bills, and this time, Margie got a ten-dollar bill! Then they all went up to the front and arranged the baskets along the edge of the podium. But they didn't turn away to their seats yet. Each one stayed and put some money into his or her own basket. Then, smiling, they all went back to their seats.

That week, the kids decided that God wasn't the only one who liked cheerful givers. They liked being cheerful givers! And Anna and Mikey's family kept coming to church, and learned all about tithe and offering, and all the ways we steward God's stuff God's way.

 Thought Question: *Do you give an offering in addition to your tithe? Do you like being a cheerful giver?*

Penny's Scholarship Fund

You might begin by saying something like, "You remember, don't you, that ten percent of our money (which is all really God's money anyway) is returned to Him as tithe? After we've done that, we can choose to give an offering. Here is a story about a girl who decides that sometimes giving is more important than receiving."

This story is suitable for children of any age.

Penny loved Wednesday better than any other day of the week. Every Wednesday, at exactly 12:00, her grandpa arrived to pick her up for their "date." First he took her to a restaurant for lunch. He would take her to nice, grown-up places, where she had to mind her manners—but because she was with her grandpa, Penny didn't mind.

After they ate, they went somewhere special. Sometimes they visited the zoo, where Penny couldn't decide whether she loved the monkeys or the penguins best. The penguins were really fun to watch, sliding down snow banks on their bellies and splashing into the cold water, or waddling around on land like stuffed animals that had come to life. On the other hand, some of the mama monkeys had babies now, and that was really cool!

Other times they went to a museum. Penny thought the one with lots of paintings in it was pretty boring, but there was a history museum with an awesome doll house with ten rooms and the nicest tiny furniture you could imagine, not to mention life-sized models of people wearing funny old-fashioned clothes. And there was a science one, where there was always something interesting to do, like dig bones out of a sand pile, figure out a math puzzle on one of the computer screens, or walk inside a giant model of a stomach.

Finally, Grandpa and Penny would go back home, where she would tell her mom stories about their day. Wednesday was Penny's favorite day!

On the other hand, she loved Sabbath pretty well, too. On Sabbath she got to see her friends in Sabbath School, and sing fun songs, and make paintings of Bible scenes. Penny loved to paint. She was thinking about being an artist someday. Then, on Sabbath afternoons, her mom would get out special games and toys Penny couldn't play with any other time, and they'd listen to special music, and eat special food, and lots of things like that. Sometimes they'd have company, and sometimes they'd go to visit the people in a nursing home and sing songs to them. Penny would take paintings to give the people, and they always loved them.

So Sabbath was pretty cool, too.

Penny didn't know that Sabbaths and Wednesdays were about to meet in a way that would be kind of hard for her.

One week at church, there was a missionary. A real, live missionary who told people about God's love! But Mrs. Bellamy didn't work in Africa or India. She wasn't on one of those islands far out in the ocean. No, Mrs. Bellamy worked in one of the big cities right here in America, and during the sermon time, she told the church about the people she worked with.

"They're wonderful, loving people," she said. "They want to be able to do something to help the world be a better place, but it's very hard for them to go to college and get good jobs. Many of them can't find work at all, or the work they get is hard and doesn't pay much. I know a lot of mothers who don't have a dad in the home to help them, and many of them work two or three jobs and hardly see their kids. The kids are in unsafe daycare situations, or they just play on the street. When there are men in the families, if they don't have steady jobs, they might go to certain corners to stand and wait, hoping for day work. A truck will come, and a man will say, 'We need six men to paint.' Fifteen men hurry forward, but they take the first six. The rest have to wait for other chances. And of course, only the young, strong-looking ones get chosen, and the work only lasts for a day or two, maybe a week."

Mrs. Bellamy showed them pictures on the screen of big, ugly apartment buildings with broken windows and dirty sidewalks. There were streets full of trash, and children playing among the piles of garbage. After she was through talking, the pastor had a special offering for the people in the city, and Penny wished she had brought more than her Sabbath School money.

But her mom invited Mrs. Bellamy to come home and eat with them! Some other families came, too, and Mrs. Bellamy told more stories about children who wanted to go to school to be doctors or teachers or business people, but knew they would be lucky to get jobs in gas stations or fast food restaurants.

"I'd like to start a scholarship fund for them," said Mrs. Bellamy. She explained that a scholarship fund was a way of saving money to send kids to college. "And in the meantime, we're trying to get enough tutors to help them get through elementary school and high school with good grades. The main thing is for them to learn to believe in themselves and know that they really can succeed. When they find out that God made them, knows them by name, and loves them, you wouldn't believe how much that helps!"

Penny said suddenly, "I wish I could help!"

"Me, too!" echoed several other children.

"Well, you can help," said Mrs. Bellamy. "First of all, the very most important thing is to pray—and everybody can do that! Then, you know you can give money, too. Even if it's only a little bit, all of our dimes and quarters add up, and God blesses them."

Penny knew that was true, and she went to get her bank and give all $13 to Mrs. Bellamy for the city children. But she wanted to do more than that. She knew stewardship was taking care of God's stuff God's way, and she knew for sure that children belong to God and that He wants all of us to take care of all the children all the time!

She thought and thought about it over the next few days. How could she get some money? She was pretty small for doing jobs. Could she sell something? She looked around her room, but didn't have any ideas.

Wednesday came, and Grandpa came to get her for their date. Penny was thinking about the children, and she wondered if they had grandpas to do things with. What if they didn't? She watched Grandpa pay for their food and leave a tip for the waiters, and an idea began to form in her mind. But she wasn't sure she liked it.

After lunch, Grandpa said, "I have something special planned for today. There is a special children's concert downtown this afternoon. Do you think you'd like that?"

"Yes, please," said Penny, but she was still thinking. After a while, she asked, "Grandpa, how much will the concert cost?"

"It's $12 for me, and $5 for you, why?" asked Grandpa.

Penny told him about the children and all the things Mrs. Bellamy had told them. "I wish I had money to give them, and…" she could hardly go on. It would be really hard! Finally, she blurted, "I was just thinking that if we don't go on our dates, we could give that money for those kids!" She blinked really fast so the tears she could feel in her eyes wouldn't fall out.

Grandpa knelt down and put his arms around her. "Why, Penny, I am so proud of you! What a loving thing to do, to be willing to give up your fun so other people can have a better life! Jesus is very happy right now. I'll tell you what. I have an idea. We don't have to give up our dates. We can go to the beach, or walk in the woods, or play on the playground, or even walk in the mall and look at the books in the bookstore. That wouldn't cost any money. Then we can give the money we would have spent to your kids and their scholarship. What do you think of that?"

Penny hugged Grandpa really tightly. "I think it would be great!" she exclaimed.

"And," added Grandpa, "once a month we'll still eat out or go to a museum or something like that. It'll be my thank you gift for you because I think you're a smart and loving little girl."

"And I think you're the best grandpa in the world!" said Penny.

Together, they both said, "I love you!"

 Thought Question: *What would you be willing to give up so that other children could have a better life?*

He Will Forgive Our Sins

You might begin by saying something like, "Stewardship is taking care of God's stuff God's way. One of the most important ways we can take care of each other and all His people is to tell everybody about God and His love. Here is a story about a boy who realizes he knows something his friend needs to know."

This story is best suited for school-aged children.

"Fight! Fight! Fight!"

Kids were running across the playground and screaming. Teachers were blowing whistles and running, too. Toby stayed out of the way and wished again that he could go to church school. He hoped stuff like this didn't happen there.

After a few minutes, the mob of kids scattered, the noise level dropped, and two teachers came across the playground, walking on either side one particular boy. Toby was upset to see that it was actually his friend, Micah! Micah had blood dripping from his nose, and one eye looked like it was going to be black in the morning. Toby walked closer, but the teachers looked mad, so he was afraid to get too close. He would talk to Micah after school.

After his last class, Toby hung around in the hallway, waiting for Micah. They were one grade apart in school, so they weren't in the same class, and they didn't get to see each other that much anymore. Pretty soon he saw Micah coming down the hall, his head hanging. He'd been cleaned up, of course, but his eye looked pretty bad. Toby called, "Hey, Micah!"

Micah looked up. "Hi," he said, but he didn't smile.

Toby walked beside him. "Are you okay?"

"Yeah," said Micah.

"What happened, anyway?"

"That jerk, Alex, called me a name."

Toby didn't point out that Micah had just called Alex a name, too. He didn't know what to say, so he didn't say anything.

After a minute, Micah continued, in a quieter voice, "I lost my temper. Again. I keep saying I'm not going to do it again, but I always do."

Toby tried to imagine what would happen if he went home with a black eye. "What are your mom and dad going to say?"

Micah shrugged, looking angry. "My dad doesn't even live with us right now. He won't care."

Toby hoped Micah's dad would care, but he didn't say that, either. "What about your mom?"

"She'll cry. She always does. She'll say it's all her fault."

"Her fault!"

"Yeah, she says she didn't raise me right, or something. But it's my fault. It's always my fault. I'm just no good."

They were outside by now, and Toby stopped and stared at Micah. "What do you mean, you're no good?"

"Just what I said. I'm no good and I never will be. I heard my uncle say that to my mom once."

Toby was amazed, and not in a good way. "Your uncle said that about you?!"

"Sure. He was right. I try, but I might as well give up. I just get so mad."

"I bet so!" said Toby. He'd get mad, too, if people talked about him like that. His own family! He felt a little nervous to ask the next question that came to his mind, but he thought this was really important. So he took a deep breath and asked, "Did you ever try asking God to help you?"

It was Micah's turn to stop walking. "God?" He sounded like he'd never heard of such a thing.

"Yeah, God says He'll help us."

"You, maybe," said Micah, walking on. "God wouldn't do anything for somebody like me."

"Oh, yeah?" said Toby. "Well, it just so happens that Jesus picked out two brothers who had a problem with their temper to be His followers!"

Micah stared. "He did? How do you know?"

"It says so in the Bible. Can you come to my house tonight? I'll show you. I'll show you some other stuff, too."

Micah hesitated. "Maybe. Could I come with you now and call my mom from your house?"

"Sure. Here's my mom's car. I'll ask."

So the two boys rode home with Toby's mom and Micah borrowed their phone. Toby took his mom in the kitchen and whispered a little bit of the story to her. "I want to try to help him, Mom."

Mom hugged him. "I'll pray with you." Then she turned to Micah and asked, "May I talk to your mother when you're through?" Toby wasn't very surprised to hear his mom asking Micah's mom if she wanted to come to their house for supper.

He took Micah up to his room and got out his Bible.

"You have your very own Bible? Wow. Can you understand it?" asked Micah.

"Sure. It's in an easy version. Look, I'll show you how I look stuff up online if I don't know where it's found. I know that two of Jesus' followers were called the 'sons of thunder' because they had bad tempers." Toby put the phrase "sons of thunder" into a Bible search engine and showed Micah Mark 3:17, which talked about James and John.

"But Jesus loved them anyway, and chose them to be His followers. Then, look here. Years and years later, one of them, John, wrote a letter we call 1 John. In 1 John 1:9, he said this."

Toby read the verse from his Bible, letting Micah look with him.

"'But God is faithful and fair. If we admit that we have sinned, he will forgive us our sins. He will forgive every wrong thing we have done. He will make us pure' (NIRV). And John ought to know, don't you think, Micah?" Toby looked at his friend.

"Did John stop losing his temper?" asked Micah.

"Not right away. I think there was a time even after he was Jesus' follower that he tried to call down fire on some people he disagreed with."

For the first time that day, Micah grinned. "I'd like to be able to do that sometimes."

Toby grinned back. "But Jesus told him to stop it, and the thing is, when he hung around Jesus a lot, it changed him. You could do that, you know."

"Do what? Hang around Jesus?"

"Yeah. It's not exactly the same now, because we can't see Him, but you can pray to Him every day, and read the Bible, and tell Jesus you're sorry and ask Him to help you not to lose your temper anymore."

"I don't have a Bible," said Micah.

Toby only thought a second. "You can have mine. We have lots of Bibles at my house."

"I can? Really? Thanks!" They heard the front door opening downstairs, and voices. "It's my mom. Hey, Mom, look! Toby gave me his Bible, and he says Jesus can help me with my temper!"

The boys ran down the stairs. Their mothers were smiling.

 Thought Question: *Have you ever tried to help a friend to understand how much God loves him or her?*

Love in Action

You might begin by saying something like, "Stewardship is taking care of God's stuff God's way. One of the most important ways we can possibly take care of each other and all His people is to tell everybody about God and His love. Here is a story about a girl who realizes she knows something her friend needs to know."

This story is best suited for school-aged children.

Tiffany was running across the playground when she heard a funny sound. She stopped and listened. It sounded like somebody crying! She looked around. Was it coming from behind the big pine tree? Tiffany walked closer and looked behind the thick, green branches. It was Ellen, the new girl.

Ellen had her head on her arms and didn't know anyone was looking at her. Tiffany knew she wouldn't want anyone to watch her crying. Should she say something, or just go away? She didn't know Ellen. Maybe she would be embarrassed. Just then, Ellen lifted her head and saw her.

Tiffany said, "Um, hi, sorry, I didn't mean to...are you okay?"

Ellen rubbed her eyes and sniffled. Tiffany remembered that she had tissues in her pocket, so she handed some to Ellen.

"Thanks," said Ellen, trying to stop crying.

"I don't mean to be nosy," said Tiffany. "Is something wrong?"

"I don't like it here," said Ellen. "Nobody likes me."

Tiffany sat down. "Well, nobody really knows you yet," she said, but she felt bad. She had to admit that she hadn't made any effort to be friendly to Ellen or to her brother, Monty. They had moved to the town just a couple of weeks before, and had to come to a new school in the middle of the year. That must be pretty hard.

"I guess I wouldn't like it, either, if I suddenly had to move away and go to a different school," Tiffany continued. "Did you like your old school?"

"Yeah. I had friends there. My mom lets me talk to them on the phone or on Skype sometimes, and we send emails and stuff. But it's not the same."

No, Tiffany knew it wasn't. "Well, we'll have to get you some friends," she said. "I'll be your friend. What kinds of things do you like to do?"

Ellen didn't seem as happy as Tiffany hoped she would be.

"Of course," she added, "it won't be the same as having your own old friends, but I think you'll like people here, too."

Ellen still hesitated. She looked at Tiffany and then looked down at the tissue she was tearing in little pieces. "It's not that," she said finally. "It's just..." She didn't seem to want to say more.

"What's the matter? You can tell me," said Tiffany.

"Well, I never went to church school before. Everything's always about God."

Tiffany just nodded. She didn't quite know what Ellen was trying to say yet.

"I'm...kind of scared of God," said Ellen.

Tiffany looked back at her, confused. "Scared of God?"

"Don't think I'm stupid or anything," muttered Ellen.

"I don't think you're stupid," Tiffany assured her. "But why are you afraid of God?"

"Well, He's always mad about something. You have to do everything right all the time, or He'll send you to...you know."

"Who told you that?" asked Tiffany.

"My friends at my other school. They said I'd hate it here because I'd have to watch what I do every second. And they're right! There are so many rules!"

Ellen looked like she might cry again.

"Well, but, the rules are to keep us all safe," said Tiffany. "Didn't your other school have rules?"

"Yeah, but...it wasn't the same. Like, if we broke the rules, we might go to the principal's office or something, but at least we wouldn't go burn forever, or anything."

"Well," said Tiffany, "first of all, God doesn't send anybody to burn forever! I can show you that in the Bible. And second of all, God loves you! Don't you know He made you and He has big plans for you? My mom said there's not a single person in the whole universe that's the same as anybody else, so God only has one of each of us! He loves you even more than your mom and dad, and you can imagine how terrible they'd feel if something bad happened to you! Would your mom burn you up?"

Ellen looked shocked. "Of course not!"

"Well, God loves you even better than that! Listen, recess is almost over. Let's go play, and then you can sit by me at art time, and after school, I'll show you some stuff in the Bible."

"Okay."

So the two girls went to play, and Tiffany introduced Ellen to all her friends. She didn't tell anybody about what they talked about, of course, because good friends keep each other's secrets. By the end of the day, Ellen felt like she was starting to have friends. And after school, Tiffany showed Ellen John 3:16 and how it said God loves the whole world.

At home, Tiffany did tell her mom about Ellen, because she knew she could trust Mom not to talk about it, and she wanted advice on good ways to help Ellen.

"Well, Tiffany, you're doing the most important thing already," said Mom.

"I am?"

"Yes. We can say that God loves people, but there's no point in the words if we don't show it. Here's another Bible verse for you."

In Tiffany's easy reading Bible, Mom looked up 1 John 3:18. Tiffany read, "Dear children, don't just talk about love. Put your love into action. Then it will truly be love" (NIRV).

"So you see," said Mom, "the main way God shows His love to us, besides all the wonderful things He does for us every day, is through each other's love. When you show love and friendship to Ellen, you are sharing God's love with her."

"Cool!" said Tiffany, and she prayed for her new friend, Ellen, that night.

The next day, the Bible lesson in school was about God's love, too. Ellen started to wonder if her old friends hadn't been right, after all. She emailed some of them about what she was learning.

Over time, Jesus got some new friends, too!

 Thought Question: What are some of the ways you share God's love with your friends?

From Timbuktu to Sabbath School

You might begin by saying something like, "When we learn to be good stewards by taking care of God's stuff God's way, it builds up God's church on earth. One of the ways we can help with this big job is to ask our friends to come to Sabbath School and church with us. Here is a story about a boy who did just that."

This story is suitable for children of any age.

Paco leaned over his handlebars and pedaled hard. Part of the way to the park was uphill, and he was always out of breath by the time he arrived. But he wanted to hurry up and get there, because Papa had said he could only stay for two hours. Paco knew two hours would go by really fast when he was playing with his friends at the park.

When he got to the park, he didn't even bother to put his bike in the bike stand—he just laid it on the grass and ran toward the climbing gym, where he could see several of his friends. Maria was sliding down the slide, and Kandy and Marcie were swinging, pumping their legs as hard as they could to see who could go higher.

Jonny and Zack were up on the top of the jungle gym, part of which was made to look like a castle. Mark was on one side, pretending he had a telescope at his eye. "I'm watching for enemy ships!" he announced to Paco, who was quickly climbing up to join them.

Across a swinging bridge, Paco's favorite part, was a platform that had a big wheel like a ship. Jonny was spinning the wheel. "I'm a pirate!" he yelled. "I'm going to shoot my cannons at your castle. Boom! Boom!"

Paco frowned a little. He had always thought these games were fun, too, but lately his Sabbath School teacher had asked them to think about what Jesus would do. Paco and his big brother, Pedro, had decided that when Jesus was a kid, they didn't think He pretended to kill people.

Zack was pretending to shoot back at Joey. "Bang, bang, you're dead!" he yelled.

"I am not, you missed!" Jonny yelled back.

"You never play fair!" shouted Zack.

That was the other problem, Paco thought. He had noticed that pretend fights often led to real ones.

"Hey, you guys," he said, "let's play explorer. We can take our ship to Timbuktu!"

Jonny and Zack stopped yelling and looked at him. "Where's Timbuktu?"

Paco grinned and shrugged. "I don't know, but it sounds cool. Maybe there's a castle there. We can pretend there is."

Jonny spun the ship wheel. "Okay, I'm the Captain and everybody has to obey me. We're going to Timbuktu now!" He made engine noises with his mouth.

"Well, I'm the king of the castle," retorted Zack. "I don't have to obey you!"

"That's okay," said Paco, crossing the hanging bridge. "I'll be your first mate, Jonny. Come on, let's sail to the castle. Look, there's the river that leads up to it. Ahoy there, King of the Golden Castle of Timbuktu! Permission to land and visit your domain!"

Zack made a grand gesture. He had a pretend cloak and sword and crown now. "You may come," he said in a kingly voice. "What land do you come from?"

"We come from, um…" Jonny looked at Paco.

"We come in the name of the King of Spain!" said Paco. "Habla español?"

"Very funny!" said Zack, and they all laughed. He got his kingly voice back and said, "I am seeking knights to serve in my army. I am about to go to war against those natives over there." He waved toward the girls on the swings.

Paco sighed. "Why do you always want to play war games?" he asked. "No matter what we do it seems like it turns into a battle!"

"Because it's fun!" said Jonny.

"Yeah," Zack agreed. "Why don't you ever want to have any fun?"

"What's so fun about pretending to kill people?" Paco asked. "I think exploring is way cooler. We could climb down this mountain the castle is on and hike over there to the jungle." He pointed to three trees nearby where they often climbed and tried hanging upside down by their knees. "I'll bet there are polar bears and tigers and giant snakes."

"But you used to like to play war," said Zack. "Why don't you want to do it anymore?"

"Because," said Paco, "our teacher at Sabbath School told us to ask ourselves what Jesus would do. I don't think He would pretend to kill people."

"What's Sabbath School?" asked Jonny.

Paco looked surprised. "Don't you know? It's the kid class, when you go to church."

"Oh, you mean like Sunday School."

"Right, except we go on Saturday because it's the seventh day and that's when God said to do it."

"I go to Sunday School with my grandma sometimes," said Jonny.

"Not me," said Zack. "What do you do there?"

"All kinds of cool stuff!" said Paco. "We sing songs and learn about Jesus and read the Bible, and do crafts. Also, we learn about stewardship, which is taking care of God's stuff God's way. That includes people." He grinned. "I'm pretty sure God doesn't want us killing His people, even pretend. Hey, do you guys want to come with me?"

"Maybe. I'll ask my mom," said Zack.

"I don't know," said Jonny.

But Paco was really happy that week when both of his friends ended up visiting Sabbath School with him. And do you know what? They started asking about what Jesus would do, too! They found out there were lots of fun things to do besides play war. And the friendship among the three boys grew and grew. Pretty soon, their moms and dads visited the church. Who knows? Maybe they'll join someday!

 Thought Question*: Which friend or friends would you like to invite to visit Sabbath School with you?*